Jewish Values in Psychotherapy

Essays on Vital Issues on the Search for Meaning

Rabbi Levi Meier, Ph.D.

Lanham • New York • London

Library of Congress Cataloging-in-Publication Data

Meier, Levi.
Jewish values in psychotherapy.

Bibliography: p.
Includes index.
1. Psychotherapy—Religious aspects—Judaism.
2. Judaism and psychology. 3. Death—Religious aspects—
Judaism. 4. Jewish law—Psychological aspects. I. Title.
BM538.P68M45   1988   296.3'875   88–178 CIP
ISBN 0–8191–6928–5 (alk. paper)
ISBN 0–8191–6929–3 (pbk. : alk. paper)

All University Press of America books are produced on acid-free
paper which exceeds the minimum standards set by the National
Historical Publications and Records Commission.

Dedication

To my Father, of blessed memory, and my Mother

Acknowledgements

I wish to express my sincere appreciation and gratitude to my professors, colleagues, friends and family who have critically read portions of this book and offered valuable suggestions. They are: Erwin Altman, J.D., of blessed memory; Manfred Altman, J.D.; Rabbi Reuven P. Bulka, Ph.D.; Rabbi Elliot Dorff, Ph.D.; Rabbi David Ellenson, Ph.D.; Rabbi David Fox, Ph.D.; Lewis Van Gelder, M.L.S.; Paula Van Gelder, M.L.S.; Jonathan Kellerman, Ph.D.; my brother, Rabbi Menahem Meier, Ph.D.; Fred Rosner, M.D.; Zanwil Sperber, Ph.D.; J. Marvin Spiegelman, Ph.D.; and Kathleen M. Wulf, Ph.D.

Cedars-Sinai Medical Center has served as the optimal setting for the integration of psychology and Judaism in the healing of patients. The Board of Directors, Board of Governors and administration have graciously facilitated the spiritual care, pastoral counseling, Jewish Medical Ethics conferences, and the Psychology and Judaism conferences of the Chaplaincy Department. Joye L. Nunn-Hill and Denise M. Kurushima of the Word Processing Center deserve recognition for their meticulous and careful production of the final work.

My wife, Marcie, has created a loving and warm atmosphere in our home, one that is conducive to genuine dialogues, creative exchanges and scholarships. Her devotion and guidance have been special sources of inspiration. Our children, Chana, Yosef Asher, Malka Mindel and Yitzchak Shlomo have stimulated us to try to create a better world for tomorrow for all of humanity. They have enriched our lives immeasurably.

The dedication of this book to my father, Alfred Meier, of blessed memory, and my mother, Frieda Meier, is a symbolic gesture of my profound love and admiration for my parents.

Permissions

Sincere gratitude to the following for permission to reprint the following articles:

Meier, L. (1986). "Psycho-Halakhic Man of Conscience," Journal of Psychology and Judaism, Volume 10 (2). Expanded version is reprinted.

Meier, L. (1986). "A Modern Jew in Search of a Soul," A Modern Jew in Search of a Soul. (Eds.). J. Marvin Spiegelman and Abraham Jacobson. Phoenix, Arizona: Falcon Press. Revised Title.

Meier, L. (1981 and 1988). "Coping with Suffering: Job, Judaism and Jung," Harvest. 27. London: Analytical Psychology Club. Part I. and in "Catholicism and Jungian Psychology," (Forthcoming). (Ed.). J. Marvin Spiegelman. Phoenix and Los Angeles: Falcon Press. Part I and Part II.

Meier, L. (1986). "Quality of Life," Jewish Values in Bioethics. New York: Human Sciences Press. Introduction.

Meier, L. (1987). "Does Death Confer Meaning on Life? A Psycho-Biblical Approach," Journal of Psychology and Judaism, Volume 11(2).

Altman, E. (1987). "Reflections on this Thing and No-Thing Called Life and Death," Journal of Psychology and Judaism, (Ed.). L. Meier. Volume 11(2), (c) Erwin Altman.

vii

Contents

Page

Foreword

The relationship between Judaism and Psychology is age old, with what have become well entrenched psychological categories already in evidence in Biblical and Talmudic tradition.

In more recent times, Psychoanalysis was condemned as "Jewish Science" even though some of the great thinkers in that school were skeptical at best about religion in general, and often quite negative about Judaism in particular.

Over the course of the past few decades, and most notably in the past decade, a concerted effort has been launched to more soberly and thoughtfully examine the links between Psychology and Judaism.

This examination has taken various forms. On the one hand, various psychological systems have been placed through a microscope against the background of Judaic thought. Some schools do better than others in this analysis. Generally, with exception, the technique components of therapy fit in quite comfortably in the Judaic context, but the philosophy and values of many therapeutic systems are found wanting, sometimes even antithetical to Judaism.

On the other hand, psychological insights have themselves provided a more profound understanding of the rationale in some Judaic norms and values. They have also provided a serious challenge to some of Judaism's most hallowed assumptions, up to and including belief in God.

In addition to these modes of study, much serious thought has started to filter through in the attempt to formulate a distinctly Judaic approach to the clinical encounter. This has usually involved separating technique from philosophy, and buffering the technique with Judaically oriented values. Or, it has taken the route of extending Judaic thought categories into the clinical realm.

Much of the literature in this ever expanding and exciting field has appeared in the pages of the Journal of Psychology and Judaism, which I have been privileged to edit since its inception in 1976. The contributions of Moshe HaLevi Spero, the Journal Overseas Editor, to the Psychology-Judaism dialectic are quite remarkable, both in quantity and quality.

Another individual who has made significant contributions to this dialogue is Levi Meier. His efforts have been expressed in many languages - the practical, the organizational, and the intellectual.

xi

Practically, Dr. Meier has served, with distinction, as the Jewish Chaplain of Cedars-Sinai Medical Center in Los Angeles. There he has employed an interesting fusion of Judaic values and psychological wisdom to the benefit of the many patients he has cared for with uncommon devotion.

Organizationally, Dr. Meier has been responsible for setting into motion an annual Psychology-Judaism conference at the Cedars-Sinai, with over two hundred participants the norm for attendance, and useful interchange on topics of importance the norm for conversation. The main papers of these conferences become special issues of the Journal of Psychology and Judaism, under Dr. Meier's guest editorship.

Intellectually, Dr. Meier has written many insightful pieces that have added appreciable insight. The first piece he wrote for the Journal of Psychology and Judaism was a masterful analysis of measurable psychological factors relative to the Biblical command to honor one's parents. Since then, a steady stream of articles and edited books on timely and timeless topics has poured forth from his pen.

In the volume, the reader is treated to the threefold dimension of Dr. Meier's Psychology-Judaism insight. Practical insight from his day-to-day experience, the fruits of his organizational endeavors, and thoughts reaped from his intellectual fertility are fused into a volume of broad scope and profound meaning. Issues of life and death are approached in a Judaically sensitive and humane way.

In reading the volume, one cannot help but feel that this sensitivity and humaneness is evidenced not only in what the author writes, but also in who the author is.

Rabbi Reuven P. Bulka, Ph.D.

Preface

Every religious behavior, thought and experience contains psychological underpinnings. A fusion of psychological and religious dimensions enhances each domain and creates a psycho-religious way of being. This psycho-religious sphere is unique in that it encompasses not only religious law but also philosophical and theological concepts. The psycho-religious or more specifically, the psycho-Judaic framework strives for the interrelatedness of diverse but complementary considerations in the search for meaning. An integrated study of all these aspects leads to a comprehensive understanding of the psychodynamics of religious behavior and thought.

The interface between religion and psychology represents the dynamic dialectic between revelatory Divine truths and subjective experience and understanding of life. This dialectic finds its synthesis in the human psyche, which attempts to bridge the unfathomable gap of the humanity-Divinity union.

The basis of all these essays is the exploration of the role of conscience within a religion that is ultimately based on Divine revelation. Furthermore, the interrelationship of faith and doubt is explored through accounts of encounters with suffering and death. The loneliness of the Jew is examined as a necessary phase in the development of the ultimate togetherness of all of humanity. The analysis of dreams serves as the unfolding of unconsciousness into consciousness. This psycho-Judaic framework encourages one to strive for the search for meaning in life.

Introduction

This introductory text explores the interrelationship of two distinct, yet complementary disciplines, Judaism and psychology.

While the subject matters of Judaism and psychology significantly overlap, their methodologies are antithetical to one another. The methodology of studying Judaism and of living as an observant Jew is ultimately based on an axiomatic belief in Divine revelation, a textual study of the Bible, Mishnah, Midrash and Talmud, traditions, customs and mores, and the creative reinterpretations of primary sources so that they apply to contemporary life. Psychology, on the other hand, is the study of human behaviors, feelings and thoughts and their interrelatedness to the totality of environment, family and humanity. Psychology is explored both by scientific experimentation and by probing one's subjective experience of life.

The religious person's life is similar to a pendulum, swaying to and fro, between diametrically opposed epistemological modes. This process represents a creative struggle in which every religious person is constantly engaged.

This collection of essays explores issues of conscience; the relationships of death to life; dreams; responses to suffering; faith and doubt; loneliness; and the ultimate harmony between psychology and religion. Clinical illustrations demonstrate one's unlimited potential for psycho-spiritual growth.

PART I

On Conscience

CHAPTER 1

Psycho-Halakhic Man of Conscience

Conscience

In the fall of 1985, I offered a course at the Jewish Studies Institute of Yeshiva University of Los Angeles entitled "Conscience and Autonomy within Jewish Tradition." Although the course contained readings from such seminal modern Orthodox Jewish philosophers and theologians as Rabbi Joseph Soloveitchik, Rabbi Samuel Belkin, Rabbi Aharon Lichtenstein, Rabbi Eliezer Berkovits, and Rabbi David Hartman, what ultimately proved most significant were the comments of students and colleagues who chose not to enroll in the course.

Their remarks reflected two stimulating and provocative areas of thought. One was that the subject matter to be taught constituted an area that it was best not to explore in serious and systematic fashion; that it was a "road less traveled," (Peck, 1979) posing the same risks as an investigation into Pardes. Pardes literally means "paradise" and figuratively refers to philosophy and mysticism. The Talmud (Hagigah 14b) relates the story of four great Rabbis, Rabbis Akiba, Ben Zoma, Ben Azzai, and Aher, who engaged in esoteric studies in the second century c.e. These four were said to have "entered paradise." Ben Azzai studied mysticism and died, Ben Zoma "saw" and lost his reason, and Aher became an apostate. Only Rabbi Akiba entered in peace and came out in peace (Scholem, 1965, p. 57). My would-be students apparently felt that a study of "Conscience and Autonomy within Jewish Tradition" was potentially too intimidating a task to undertake, bearing too much similarity to an inquiry into Pardes (Linzer, 1984, chapter 1).

The other reason behind the students' reluctance to enroll in my course was that they were convinced a priori that anyone who genuinely explored the issue of conscience could not maintain his traditional Jewish practices and beliefs. They believed that Judaism does not allow for one's individual conscience to be expressed.

This introductory investigation hopes to demonstrate not only that conscience is discussed within the Jewish tradition, but that it forms an essential aspect of Jewish thought. The centrality of conscience is most poignantly expressed by R. Aryeh Leib Heller in the introduction to his Kezot ha-Hoshen, an eighteenth century study on civil, economic, and legal

3

jurisprudence as outlined in the Code of Jewish Law (Karo, Shulhan Arukh, Hoshen Mishpat):

"The Torah was not given to angels (Talmud, Berakhot 25b), but to human beings who have been endowed with human faculties and abilities."

Rabbi Heller emphasized the paradoxical aspect of Judaism. Judaism, a divinely revealed religion, can only be comprehended via human understanding. This paradox of the interrelatedness of Divinity-humanity constitutes the core issue underlying conscience.

What is conscience? And what is the relationship of conscience to a revealed religion?

The unabridged edition of the Random House Dictionary of the English Language defines conscience as "the sense of what is right or wrong in one's conduct or motives, impelling one toward right action" (Stein, 1967). No Jewish encyclopedia has an entry on "conscience." Conscience is covered in most standard encyclopedias, with the Encyclopedia of Religion and Ethics (1952) devoting part of its general article on conscience to the place of this concept within Judaism. The article, however, is a general exposition of Jewish ethics, as if ethics and conscience were identical.

Is a sense of what is right or wrong derived from a Divinely revealed Torah, or from an autonomous self? Assuming that a sense of right and wrong is derived from the Torah, what was the source of right and wrong prior to revelation?

The Midrash comments that Noah, Abraham, Isaac, and Jacob observed the commandments of the Torah (Midrash Rabbah, Genesis 26:5;32:5). Whether this Midrash is to be understood literally or figuratively is a moot point (Heineman, 1954, p. 106). However, it is clear that most people who lived prior to the revelation were not endowed with sufficient intuitive ability to observe by their own initiative the ethical commandments of the Torah as were Noah, Abraham, Isaac, and Jacob. How, then, did other people develop a sense of what was right?

The Talmud states: "Rabbi Yohanan observed: if the Torah had not been given, we could have learned modesty from the cat, honesty from the ant, chastity from the dove, and good manners from the cock" (Talmud, Erubin 100b). This significant passage implies that a sense of right and wrong not only predates revelation, but that it is an inherent part of a more universal revelation - that of the creation of the world. Through nature, man can learn virtuous behavior.

4

The Rabbis of the Mishnah recognized that natural morality has always existed.

The Mishnah states: "Rabbi Elazar ben Azariah says: if there is no Torah there is no Derekh Eretz (natural morality) and without natural morality there is no Torah" (Mishnah, Abot 3:17). The Hebrew expression Derekh Eretz literally means "the way of the land," and refers to all the things which are necessary for the sustenance of life. Therefore, Derekh Eretz at times could refer to professionalism or sexual relations or general worldliness or social mores or ethics and morality. Rabbi Samson Raphael Hirsch defines Derekh Eretz as encompassing:

> ... the situations arising from and dependent upon the circumstance that the earth is the place where the individual must live, fulfill his destiny and dwell together with others and that he must utilize resources and conditions provided on earth in order to live and to accomplish his purpose. Accordingly, the term Derekh Eretz is used primarily to refer to ways of earning a living, to the social order that prevails on earth, as well as to the mores and considerations of courtesy and propriety arising from social living and also to things pertinent to good breeding and general education. (Hirsch, 1978, p. 434)

In this context, Rabbenu Yonah interprets Derekh Eretz as referring to ethical virtues and morality (Mishnah, Abot 3:17).

Natural morality and Torah complement one another. Although both co-exist and enhance one another in guiding mankind toward ethical behavior, each domain exists independently of the other as well.

The Midrash states: "Rabbi Yishmael, the son of Rabbi Nachman said: for twenty-six generations, Derekh Eretz (natural morality) preceded the Torah" (Midrash Rabbah, Leviticus 9:3). The twenty-six generations refer to the span of time from the creation of the world until the giving of the Torah. This statement implies that natural morality not only existed prior to revelation but also forms the basis of the Torah.

In reflecting on man's search for what is right or wrong, it is axiomatic that man prior to revelation and man post-revelation have had the same opportunity to live an ethical life. It is logically and philosophically untenable to assume that God could create a potentially more meaningful life or a potentially more ethical way of living for one period in human history than for a prior epoch in that history.

5

If man's conscience assisted him in his search for what was good, why was revelation necessary at all? Furthermore, has the function of conscience been superseded by Divine revelation? What is the role of conscience in the post-revelation period? Does conscience conflict with Jewish Law or complement it?

My thesis is that conscience complements Jewish Law. A manifestation of the complementary nature of conscience to Jewish thought and law is the concept of Lifnim Mishurat Hadin, a mode of behavior that goes "beyond the letter of the law." The Torah anticipates that there will arise occasions upon which mankind will be required to pursue higher moral standards and guide itself by an even nobler mode of conduct than that which is prescribed in the Torah itself (Spero, 1983, p. 167; Shilo, 1978; Berman, 1977, 1975).

Nahmanides comments on "And you shall do what is right and good in the eyes of God:"

> Our Rabbis have a beautiful Midrash on this verse. They have said: ["that which is right and good"] refers to a compromise, and going beyond the requirement of the letter of the law. The intent of this is as follows: At first he [Moses] stated that you are to keep His [God's] statutes and His testimonies which He commanded you; and now He is formulating that even where He has not commanded you, you must give thought as well to do what is good and right in His eyes, for He loves the good and the right.

> Now this is a great principle, for it is impossible to mention in the Torah all aspects of man's conduct with his neighbors and friends, and all his various transactions, and the ordinances of all societies and countries. But since He mentioned many of them - such as, "Thou shalt not go up and down as a talebearer; Thou shalt not take vengeance, nor bear any grudge; neither shalt Thou stand idly by the blood of Thy neighbor; Thou shalt not curse the deaf; Thou shalt rise up before the hoary head," and the like - He reverted to state in a general way that in all matters, one should do what is good and right, including even compromise and going beyond the requirements of the law.

> Other examples are the Rabbis' ordinances concerning the prerogative of a neighbor, and even what they said [concerning the desirability] that one's youthful reputation be unblemished, and that one's conversation

6

with people be pleasant. Thus [a person must seek to refine his behavior] in every form of activity, until he is worthy of being called "good and upright." (Nahmanides, Deuteronomy 6:18)

Nahmanides reiterates this notion in his comments on "You shall be holy:"

> Therefore, after having listed the matters which He prohibited altogether, Scripture followed them by a general command that we practice moderation even in matters which are permitted....Similarly, he [man] should keep himself away from impurity [in his ordinary daily activity], even though we have not been admonished against it in the Torah. ...And such is the way of the Torah, that after it lists certain specific prohibitions, it includes them all in a general precept.
>
> Thus, after warning with detailed laws regarding all business dealings between people, such as not to steal or rob or to wrong one another, and other similar prohibitions, He said in general: 'And Thou shalt do that which is right and good,' thus including under a positive commandment the duty of doing that which is right, and of agreeing to a compromise [when not to do so would be inequitable]; as well as all requirements to act beyond the line of justice [i.e., to be generous in not insisting upon one's rights as defined by the strict letter of the law, but to agree to act beyond that line of the strict law].
>
> The Torah has admonished us against immorality and forbidden foods, but has permitted sexual intercourse between man and wife, and the eating of [certain] meat and wine. If so, a man of desire could consider this to be a permission to be passionately addicted to sexual intercourse with his wife or many wives, and be among wine bibbers, among gluttonous eaters of flesh, and speak freely all profanities, since this prohibition has not been [expressly] mentioned in the Torah, and thus he will become a sordid person within the permissible realm of the Torah." (Nahmanides, Leviticus, 19:2)

Both passages accentuate the fact that conducting oneself ethically requires much more than what is prescribed specifically in the Torah. Most significant, however, is that the emphasis upon transcending the normative guidelines is indeed an integral part of the Torah and Jewish law.

Conscience does not consist of a metalegal dimension but a specific legal structure.

Lifnim Mishurat Hadin has been operationalized in various ways in Talmudic literature. Following the letter of the law exclusively was ascribed as a factor leading to the destruction of Jerusalem. The Talmud states:

> 'That they shall do' - this means [acts] within the requirements of the law. For Rabbi Johanan said: Jerusalem was destroyed only because they gave judgments therein in accordance with Biblical law. Were they then to have judged in accordance with untrained arbitrators? But say thus: because they based their judgments [strictly] upon Biblical law, and did not go within the requirements of the law." (Talmud, Baba Mezia 30b)

The national calamity of the destruction of Jerusalem and the Temple was ascribed not to a lack of proper observances, but to several reasons, including mankind's acting only according to the letter of the law and not observing "beyond the letter of the law." Thus, unless conscience is acted upon, the whole raison d'etre of observant Jewish life is rendered significantly deficient. Although the Torah does not and cannot prescribe the proper dictates of the heart in all potential circumstances, the philosophy of purpose of the Torah is to create a human being who constantly seeks to uncover a higher moral or spiritual purpose (Belkin, 1978, pp. 14-19).

This is indeed the meaning of the word "Torah." The Greeks (Septuagint) translated Torah as Nomos (law), "probably in the sense of a living network of traditions and customs of a people. The designation of the Torah by Nomos and by its Latin successor, lex, has historically given rise to the sad misunderstanding that Torah means legalism" (Encyclopaedia Judaica, 1971, 15:1238-1239).

Thus, Judaism was misapprehended to be primarily a religion of law. Fulfillment of proper ritual was misperceived as constituting sufficient adherence to Judaism. Torah in fact comes from the Hebrew root word which means "teaching." Teaching embodies "law and philosophy, Talmud and Bible, manifestation and essence" (Leeuw, 1938). It also encompasses norms and spirituality, theology and historical experiences, and finally, the letter of the law and the spirit of the law (conscience). The teaching of Torah must create a Jewish religious consciousness that integrates a normative legal system with spirituality, creating not a Halakhic man (Soloveitchik, 1983), but rather a Halakhic man of conscience.

8

Although Halakhah includes conscience, it nevertheless has to be accentuated as the Halakhic man of conscience.

Etymologically, the word conscience means "with knowledge." The core of conscience allows one to have a panoramic view of all knowledge, a sense of interrelatedness of knowledge, facts and emotions. This totality creates a gestalt, whereby physical, biological and psychological phenomena form a new unit.

The Halakhic man of conscience concerns himself with the process of becoming intuitively righteous. The purpose of Halakhah (Jewish law) is to serve as a means of achieving the highest human potential: Imitatio Dei, emulating God's Divine attributes or actions, including justice and mercy. This religious philosophy of purpose affords a raison d'etre to man's continued existence. The purpose of man's existence is to sanctify God by emulating Him, which makes man an associate of God.

Another operational definition of Lifnim Mishurat Hadin is exhibited in a celebrated Talmudic passage, in which following the strict law is subordinated to following the spirit of the law:

> Some porters [negligently] broke a barrel of wine belonging to Rabbah bar Hanah. Thereupon he seized their garments. So they went and complained to Rab. "Return their garments to them," he ordered. "Is that the law?," he enquired. "Yes," he rejoined: "'That thou mayest walk in the way of good men'." Their garments having been returned, they observed, "We are poor men, have worked all day, and are in need; are we to get nothing?" "Go and pay them," he ordered. "Is that the law?" he enquired. "Yes," was his reply, "'And keep the path of the righteous.'" (Talmud, Baba Mezia 83a)

Although the workers were negligent, Rab told Rabbah bar Hanah that in such a case one should not insist on the letter of the law (i.e., withhold the workers' pay). Living "beyond the letter of the law" required in this instance not only a transition to a higher standard of morality, it demanded direct opposition to the letter of the law. This episode demonstrated that acting according to one's conscience is not merely a step toward a higher level of moral conduct within the same continuum, but represents a quantum leap to a qualitatively different plane. Here the law yielded to something beyond itself -- something that could not be codified, but only perceived in the unique situation that presented itself. The

9

moral agent had to make a judgment, taking into account not only the law but also an inner voice which could not be suppressed.

Conscience focuses not on what is, but on what ought to be. Thus, conscience is essentially intuitive. Conscience manifests itself by demonstrating the interrelatedness of the totality of man's knowledge. It is the task of conscience to reveal the one course of action that is required; the unique possibility to be selected by a specific person in a specific situation. Only conscience is capable of adjusting and applying the eternal law to the specific situation in which a flesh-and-blood individual finds himself. Living one's conscience means living perpetually on a highly personalized level, aware of the full moral concreteness of each situation.

Having determined the central role of conscience and how it has been operationalized in Talmudic literature, how can one be certain that one is functioning with a pure conscience in the various situations and circumstances which confront man, rather than with an "ordinary" conscience which is not based on Torah values?

Purity of conscience may well be an impossible achievement. Man is born into a certain family, a particular culture and milieu, a specific time in history, and with very specific genetic endowments. The dictates of one's heart are inevitably influenced by all these factors and more. Family values, the special influences of the cohort generation and the limitations of the biopsychosocial conditions all play a role in the formation of conscience.

This awareness of the uniqueness of each individual human being is fundamental in understanding the special nature of every human being's conscience. The Midrash states: "Just as the physical features of everyone differ from one another, so do their values" (Midrash Rabbah, Numbers 25:11). Thus, both the physical make-up and value system of every person are different from those of every other human being.

Unlike Nahmanides, Maimonides understands the concept of Lifnim Mishurat Hadin as referring to conduct which is only applicable to an elitist pious sect. Maimonides states: "And the early pietists would incline their traits from the median path toward either extreme. One trait they would incline toward the one extreme, another toward the other extreme, and this is Lifnim Mishurat Hadin" (Mishneh Torah, Deot 1:5).

Maimonides, however, subsumes character development and ethical sensitivity under the demand of Imitatio Dei (Deuteronomy 28:9).

10

He states: "And we are commanded to walk in these median paths and they are the right and the good paths, as it is written, 'And you shall walk in His ways'" (Mishneh Torah, Deot 1:5). This passage refers to a sense of striving for an ideal, rather than of satisfying basic demands. The ethic of Imitatio Dei is not just a lofty ideal reserved for an elite, aristocratic, pious few, but a pressing obligation.

Thus, both Nahmanides and Maimonides concur on the significance of pursuing a higher universal ethic than that which is prescribed in the Torah, but differ in pinpointing the Halakhic rubric from which it springs. Nahmanides views conscience as part of the Halakhic system of Lifnim Mishurat Hadin, while Maimonides views conscience as part of the commandment of Imitatio Dei. Thus, the pursuit of a higher moral obligation is part and parcel of the Halakhic system; it is not optional, but becomes as compulsory as the legal requirements themselves. The complementary nature of conscience to law is part of the Halakhic system. The legal texts themselves introduce moral considerations into the legal process. The Halakhah also saw that the "higher law" was ordained by the law itself (Landman, 1969, pp. 18-20).

Despite the fact that law and conscience are both rooted in the Divine Halakhic system, the methods employed in arriving at a specific action within each realm proceed according to vastly different lines of reasoning.

"Law" refers to a set of statutes which regulate an individual's overall conduct by means of established behavioral guidelines. It also refers to one's expressed words, thoughts, and feelings. In contrast, "conscience" calls for thoughtful, deliberate action in a specific case under very special circumstances. In the realm of conscience, every case is phenomenologically different. The differences are so crucial that no meaningful directives can be formulated; every decision is a personal one. The "higher law" varies from individual to individual (Landman, 1969, p. 19).

In the area of conscience, the Halakhic norm becomes situational. Whether the overall guideline is Imitatio Dei or Lifnim Mishurat Hadin, it suggests a general direction and not a series of specifically prescribed acts. Conscience depends on circumstances and may vary with the individual. Since no two individuals look alike or think alike, their consciences may guide them differently depending on how each perceives reality.

Reality exists only as it is perceived by the observer. The observer is conditioned by his unique and varied background. Although the Torah's rules are absolute, Rabbinic legislation has provided latitude and flexibility by allowing

11

those who observe Jewish law to perceive reality individually and act accordingly, based on their own conscience. This fluidity of Halakhah within the domains of Imitatio Dei or Lifnim Mishurat Hadin is also demonstrated by the Rabbinic concept of "This is the law, but it is not to be publicized" (Talmud, Shabbat 12b). A Halakhic man of conscience can allow himself flexibility and leniency under specific circumstances; such decisions, however, cannot be prescribed for others.

Another example of the fluidity available to the Halakhic man of conscience is the expression, "It is different in this case," a term found in Talmudic literature thousands of times (e.g., Talmud, Baba Mezia 24a). This expression implies that even though a general rule of conduct may have been provided for certain situations, any slightly different variable within those situations -- e.g., an elderly person rather than an adult; a sick person rather than a healthy one; a drought rather than the normal amount of rain -- is sufficient reason for the Talmud to say, "It is different here." In other words, while the rule still applies in general, it does not apply in this particular case.

For example, on Yom Kippur (the Day of Atonement) a Jew must abstain from five forms of activity, including washing himself. Other than the minimal cleaning of hands and eyes, washing and bathing is prohibited. One of the categories of people exempted from this rule is a bride during her first thirty days after marriage. The importance of connubial bliss at the beginning of a new marriage permitted this (washing) leniency (Talmud, Yoma 73b), an exception clearly motivated by the communal Halakhic man of conscience.

The enhancement of human dignity, the quest for domestic peace, and the mitigation or alleviation of anxiety or pain are integral parts of the Halakhic-conscience process. These factors have not only evolved into Halakhic norms themselves, but they have done so due to the necessity of Halakhic-conscience (Lichtenstein, 1975, p.67).

Although Marvin Fox (1979) allows for the possibility of an ethic which is independent of the Halakhah, he does not accept the textual proofs of Lifnim Mishurat Hadin nor the Talmudic passage indicating that it would have been possible to imitate certain forms of animal behavior for the maintenance of an ordered society and to achieve good personal relations (Talmud, Erubin 100b; Urbach, 1969, pp. 286-287).

His objection to Lifnim Mishurat Hadin reiterates the fact that the requirement to be holy (Leviticus 19:2) is presented in the Torah as a Divine mandate. Furthermore, Nahmanides speaks explicitly of the fact that this verse is a commandment

12

(Fox, 1979, pp. 14-15). Fox's objection is valid regarding the title of Aharon Lichtenstein's (1975) essay, "Does Jewish Tradition Recognize an Ethic Independent of the Halakha?," yet it only serves to further validate that the impetus to transcend Halakhah is an indigenous aspect of the Halakhic system. "Independence of the Halakhah" is not the central consideration; the Divine mandate creating the Halakhic-conscience is compelling. Thus, the Torah recommends or even prescribes proper action even when such action may transcend and differ from the requirements of the law.

In reference to "If the Torah had not been given, we could have learned modesty from the cat..." (Talmud, Erubin 100b), Fox maintains "that this would not bring us to a knowledge of our duty to behave in this way" (Fox, 1979, p. 13). He maintains that both law and independent morality require some ground of obligation. If independent morality is based on a prudent decision, then there is no awareness of being duty bound.

However, both Saadya Gaon and Maimonides maintain that mankind would have been able to evolve a code of moral laws based on man's innate pursuit of ethical and saintly behavior. Maimonides states explicitly that someone who has no desire for shedding of blood, theft, robbery, fraud -- things which all people commonly agree are evils -- are to be more praised than he who desires these evils but restrains his passions (Twersky, 1972, p. 378; Altmann, 1969, pp. 94-105).

Thus, the contrary of Fox's contention is accurate. Independent morality meritoriously supersedes Divinely commanded ethical behavior.

Psycho-Halakhic Man

At the beginning of this essay, I referred to the essential paradox of Judaism: that although the Torah was given by God, the words of the Torah can only be understood by human beings. It has been demonstrated that the Divinity-humanity fusion creates a Halakhic man of conscience.

Not only under special circumstances, but also in fundamental basics, the Halakhic man of conscience is involved in various interpretations of the Torah. The Torah directs us to honor and give reverence to our father and mother (Exodus 20:12 and Leviticus 19:3). The Talmud defines honor as positive acts of personal service, including feeding and dressing one's parent. Reverence is defined as the avoidance of disrespectful acts; rabbinic examples include not sitting in a parent's seat or speaking before parents, and never contradicting them (Talmud, Kiddushin 31b).

13

Is the definition of a parent strictly a biological one (Talmud, Yebamot 22a and b), with no significance attached to the parenting skills one may or may not possess? Is a parent still a parent if he/she is engaged in child molestation or child abuse? What is the status of "parents" who have adopted newborn babies?

Although the Responsa literature deals with many of these questions, ultimately even the "clear" law of honoring and revering one's parents is frequently left to the realm of the Halakhic man of conscience (Blidstein, 1975). Adults who were victimized as children by their parents, for example, must necessarily differ in their response in honoring and revering their parents. Also, one's individual pain threshold plays a role. Some children, upon reaching middle-aged adulthood, may be capable of understanding that their parents were mentally ill, while others may have been hurt so badly that they are unable to perceive their parents as merely ill rather than evil.

Psychological predisposition also plays a role in the creation of the Halakhic man of conscience. Every person has an individualized psyche. This is most clearly demonstrated by giving a mental status examination to both patients and non-patients. Every person achieves a singular score in thought patterns, perceptions and affect.

Allow me, therefore, to suggest a new category of psycho-Halakhic man: the psycho-Halakhic man of conscience. While neither exclusively a psychological man nor a man of conscience, he has elements of both. He is also not exclusively a Halakhic man, although Halakhah is a primary element in his life.

Man experiences the world as a subject, as an object, and at times as a fusion of subject and object. These three different experiences of reality reflect different responses on the part of the psycho-Halakhic man of conscience.

Man-as-subject experiences the world as different from himself. The world is not the man, but at the same time the world makes sense only as it bears some relationship to man as the subject who perceives it.

Man, the subject, is located in physical space and time, and possesses desires, feelings, and fears. Man-as-subject sees objects from a point of view. He experiences life from a point of view that is limited, but it is exactly that limitation that provides a boundary offering stability and definition to experience.

As man-as-subject experiences the world each day, his experience forms a continuity with what he underwent yesterday, last year, and thirty years ago. All of this represents a point of orientation, in terms of which man-as-subject organizes and gives meaning to his experience.

A second aspect of man-as-subject involves the exercise of power in relation to the world around man. This power affords man some control over what he experiences. Man can translate his desires into changes in the world and observe the effect of his actions.

Man as subject has both an orienting point of reference and is also an active agent. Laing has stated the matter in the following way:

> I wish to define a person in a twofold way; in terms of experience, as a center of orientation of the objective universe; and in terms of behavior, as the origin of actions. Personal experience transforms a given field into a field of intention and action; only through action can our experience be transformed. (Laing, 1967, p.8)

A third aspect of man-as-subject is that of man as a party in a relationship. When someone relates to man-as-subject, man-as-subject fully understands that the other party is trying to effect a change in man-as-subject's organization of the world. Thus, man-as-subject is not only a body which communicates, but an ever-evolving consciousness concerned with how he is giving meaning to the world.

Man-as-subject does not objectify. Attributes are not given to the self in this experience; man is the "observer," not the "observed." Man-as-object, however, does objectify and assign attributes. Man-as-object is the object of attention.

The experience of man-as-subject is immediate. This man only "lives." In contrast, man-as-object is a man mediated by symbols, and he is "known" rather than "lived." Man-as-object is the experience of self-scrutinization and constant evaluation. This requires the ability to reflect upon oneself. Man-as-object is inevitable. However, when man-as-object becomes so pervasive in the experiential life of the individual that man-as-subject is eclipsed, pathology ensues.

Man-as-object has essential characteristics and experiences that define what he is. This stands in contrast to the notion of man-as-subject, which concerns itself with the more prosaic fact that man exists.

15

Man-as-subject talks in such terms as "'I' think of an idea," "'I' desire to play tennis," and "'I' fear dying."

Subjectivity itself thus turns out to be not only an intentionality -- a meaning-conferring ability -- but a relationship. It is impossible to have an objective relationship to anything at all; at the very least it would be intentional and thus subjective (Poole, 1972, p.95).

Kierkegaard stated:
> With reference to religion - subjectivity is truth. The objection to objectivity is a subjective one, coming as it does from a passionate involvement with the ethical responsibility of the thinking individual. Thinkerless thought is mere objectivity - it is a failure of responsibility.
>
> What is accepted as true is accepted as true because of an already existing structure of belief in the individual, an existing structure of interest or fear. The answer to Pilate's famous question is that there is no truth, only truths. (Kierkegaard, 1941, p. 171)

Man-as-object reflects upon our desires, fears, and thoughts. We name them, judge them, reason with regard to them and have feelings about them. With dispassionate detachment, man-as-object reflects upon himself.

The "I" experience allows for becoming, while the "objectified me" may contain aspects of bad faith (Sartre, 1956, Part 1, Chapter 2).

The psycho-Halakhic man of conscience maintains an intricate balance of subject and object. Psychopathology is manifest when man functions only as subject or only as object.

William James also integrates the objective and subjective as comprising a part of the religious man. James states that to multitudes of peoples, objective truth represents an ideal refuge. Theology has never tolerated probable truths. The multitude aspire to a dogmatic theology which is arrived at in a priori manner. Yet, James concludes:

> The world of our experience consists at all times of two parts, an objective and a subjective part, of which the former may be incalculably more extensive than the latter, and yet the latter can never be omitted or suppressed. Religion is the unique combination of objective theocentric theological truths and the subjective phenomena regarding these

truths which are expressed in terms of an anthropocentric view of life. (James, 1958, p. 377-378)

Furthermore, surveying the field of comparative religion, it is noted that although a great variety of theological and philosophical thought prevails among mankind, the human feelings engendered by religious observance are almost always the same.

Thus, the objective theories generated by religions are secondary; the essence of religion involves the more constant element and expression of feeling. James quotes Professor Leuba:

> God is not known, He is not understood; He is used - sometimes as meat-purveyor, sometimes as moral support, sometimes as friend, sometimes as an object of love. If He proves Himself useful, the religious consciousness asks for no more than that. Does God really exist? How does He exist? What is He? are so many irrelevant questions. Not God, but life, more life, a larger, richer, more satisfying life is, in the last analysis, the end of religion. The love of life, at one and every level of development, is the religious impulse. (James, 1958, p. 382)

The theocentric view of religion is significant to the degree that it has an impact on anthropocentrism.

Julius Guttmann, the distinguished scholar of Jewish philosophy, also expresses his own view on the relationship between objective Divine law and subjective man. He states that the commandments are the conduit for living a holy life. This behavior allows for religious expression of feelings as well. Furthermore, the commandments must themselves be liberated from their strictly ritualistic context and re-adapted to their original context of religious-intended behavior. At times the legalism of the law creates the artificial appearance of "religious" life (Guttmann, 1955, pp. 274-275).

Guttmann provides an example which demonstrates the subject-object dichotomy as well. Naturally, he reminds us, there is a Divine command to pray to God. However, if by chance one has forgotten to include the special "New Moon" paragraph, one is obligated to repeat one's prayer in its entirety. Guttmann maintains that such stringent requirements literally eliminate religious expression within Judaism for the

17

sake of maintaining the legal system. The underlying thesis of Guttmann's philosophy is that man must not be eliminated from the objective law.

Interestingly, Rabbinic codifiers have alluded to this concept as well. The Rabbis were asked to respond to an inquiry regarding whether a person who prays without proper religious devotion is obliged to repeat his prayers. In conceptual terminology, it would be phrased as, "Can a person fulfill his obligation to pray as a man-object (an 'I - It' relationship) without having been in the state of a man-subject (an 'I-Thou' relationship)?" The Rabbis responded that since it is nearly impossible to thrust man into an I-Thou relationship on demand, he is not obligated to repeat his prayers (Karo, Shulhan Arukh, Orach Hayyim 101:1).

Two case vignettes will concretize our theory:

> The beloved daughter of Rabbi Elijah Pruzna (Feinstein) took sick about a month before she was to be married and after a few days was rapidly sinking. Rabbi Elijah's son entered into the room where R. Elijah, wrapped in tallit and tefillin, was praying with the congregation, to tell him that his daughter was in her death throes. R. Elijah went into his daughter's room and asked the doctor how much longer it would be until the end. When he received the doctor's reply, Rabbi Elijah returned to his room, removed his Rashi's tefillin, and quickly put on the tefillin prescribed by Rabbenu Tam, for immediately upon his daughter's death, he would be an onen, a mourner whose dead relative has not as yet been buried, and as such would be subject to the law that an onen is exempt from all commandments. After he removed his second pair of tefillin, wrapped them up, and put them away, he entered his dying daughter's room, in order to be present at the moment his most beloved daughter of all would return her soul back to its Maker. We have here great strength and presence of mind, the acceptance of the Divine decree with love, the consciousness of the law and the judgment, the might and power of the Halakhah, and faith, strong like flint. (Soloveitchik, 1983, pp. 77-78)

This is an example of Rabbi Soloveitchik's view of the Halakhic-man. Does this Halakhic man allow himself to be a psycho-Halakhic man of conscience? How would the psycho-Halakhic man of conscience have reacted?

Event	Hypothesis: Man as Subject-Object psycho-Halakhic man of conscience	Hypothesis: Man as Object Halakhic man
1) Rabbi Elijah's most beloved daughter is about to be married.	1) Rabbi Elijah feels elated about the forthcoming marriage.	1) Rabbi Elijah reflects about his daughter's marriage and the meaning this has for her and her husband, as well as any implication this meaning has for him.
2) A month before the forthcoming marriage, Rabbi Elijah's daughter becomes ill.	2) Rabbi Elijah feels sad and hopes for his daughter's speedy recovery.	2) Rabbi Elijah reflects on the meaning of the juxtaposition of his daughter's illness and the forthcoming marriage.

19

Event	Hypothesis: Man as Subject-Object psycho-Halakhic man of conscience	Hypothesis: Man as Object Halakhic man
3) Her condition deteriorates rapidly.	3) Rabbi Elijah feels anger toward God.	3) Rabbi Elijah mentally disengages from his daughter's critical illness and continues his normal activity of praying with his congregation.
4) Rabbi Elijah's prayers are interrupted and he is informed that his daughter is in her death throes. Rabbi Elijah asks the doctor how much longer his daughter will live.	4) Rabbi Elijah is perplexed, confused, and cries out for help from God and asks for support from his family and friends.	4) Rabbi Elijah sees only his Halakhic reality of desiring to fulfill the will of God by putting on another pair of Tefillin before that opportunity is denied to him by his daughter's death.

Event	Hypothesis: Man as Subject-Object psycho-Halakhic man of conscience	Hypothesis: Man as Object Halakhic man
5) Rabbi Elijah puts on another pair of Tefillin and then returns to his daughter's room, at which time she dies.	5) Rabbi Elijah engages God in the issues of "Job" and feels totally isolated.	5) Rabbi Elijah ascribes meaning to his daughter's death, which is reflected by his quickly putting on his Tefillin prior to her death.

Although there may be some mutuality and overlap in events one, two, three, and four, event five diametrically distinguishes the two hypotheses. The Halakhic man acts as man-as-object; while the psycho-Halakhic man of conscience fuses the subject-object dichotomy. Rabbi Soloveitchik's view of Halakhic man is primarily that of man-as-object: Halakhic reality imposed on man's experiential reality. Man gives meaning to life's vicissitudes by submitting to the Divine Halakhic imperative.

This Divine imperative has no relationship to man's desires.

Rabbi Simeon ben Gamaliel points out:
> One should not say, 'I do not want to eat meat together with milk; I do not want to wear clothes made of a mixture of wool and linen; I do not want to enter into an incestuous marriage,' but he should say, 'I do indeed want to, yet I must not, for my Father in Heaven has forbidden it.' (Sifra, Leviticus 20:26)

Man-as-subject can also be a Halakhic man. Man-as-subject is not antithetical to Halakhic man. Man-as-subject contains the elements of the psycho-Halakhic man of conscience. This psycho-Halakhic man of conscience manifests the quintessential aspect of Imitatio Dei or Lifnim Mishurat Hadin.

Another case vignette is taken from my pastoral work as Chaplain at Cedars-Sinai Medical Center. A middle-aged woman related that as a child she had been physically and emotionally abused. As a young adult, she had decided to disengage from her mother because the abuse was still continuing, although in more subtle fashion.

21

The mother was now ill and had requested to see her daughter. The daughter, an observant Jew, presented the issue of whether, according to Jewish law, she was now obligated to visit her mother.

How would Halakhic woman respond? And how would psycho-Halakhic woman respond? Halakhic woman would be guided above all by Jewish law; whatever decision is reached is not as relevant, in this context, as how this decision was arrived at. Halakhic woman looks at absolute facts, such as:

1) a mother,
2) a daughter,
3) the existence of child abuse,
4) an emotionally ill mother,
5) a mother's request, and
6) a middle-aged child having become disengaged from her mother. The Halakhic woman fulfills the commandment of honoring one's mother and visits her mother.

Employing these criteria, the two women are perceived exclusively as objects. However, can subjectivity play a role in this Halakhic process? Can we focus on the mother and daughter not only as objects, but as subjects? Why is the mother requesting to see her daughter now? Can the mother talk to her daughter and say words to the effect that, "I'm sorry for what I did to you as a child?" Can the daughter share her dilemma with her mother? Can all these real experiences take place to bring about not a Halakhic-woman but a psycho-Halakhic woman of conscience (Blidstein, 1975, pp. 130-136)?

The psycho-Halakhic man of conscience finds his parallel and contrast in Buber's I-It and I-Thou relationship.

Buber assumes that a relationship with God is similar to a relationship with another person. You may have an I-It relationship by objectifying the other person and knowing everything about the person. Despite describing him, however, you may not know him. During this relationship you may evaluate, analyze, and even dissect the other. You may know certain things about each other, but you do not know each other.

In the I-Thou relationship, you come to know the other person through intimate communication - through dialogue. The essence of this dialogue is to establish a living mutual relationship.

The theological implication of Buber's two dichotomous relationships is his assertion that God can only be addressed in the I-Thou relationship.

22

The I-Thou relationship involves a person's whole being. The mind is not divided. It is totally man-as-subject. At the moment of the encounter, it is also exclusive. You are totally absorbed; you are your true self, with your virtues and vices, expressed thoughts and secret thoughts. No deception is possible.

This encounter takes place in the present. Relating this to God, Buber claims that you can only talk to God but not about God. Thus, every religious person has a living encounter with God. Man feels addressed by God. The individual may experience a heightened awareness of the Divine, or even an inner transformation of his being.

In contrast, however, the Halakhic man, for Buber, cannot be the conduit for an I-Thou encounter. Buber espouses "the living deed that binds man to God" (Buber, 1967, p.45). By "the living deed," Buber means an effort "to restore to the deed the freedom and sanctity diminished by the stern rule of the ritual law, and to release it from the straits of prescriptions that had become meaningless, in order to free it for the holiness of an active relationship with God, for a religiosity of the deed" (Buber, 1967, p.46).

Buber emphasizes the encounter, the concrete life-situation of the individual. For Buber, there are no rules or prescriptions which can prepare an individual for these concrete encounters (Kaufman, 1976, p.71-72). Thus, for Buber there exists a "psycho-conscience man," without the Halakhically - externalized objectified prescriptions. The "I" who performs the Divine commandments always does so as a partner with the "Thou," not as an isolated individual. Naturally, people cannot remain in the I-Thou state, but must spend most of their lives in the I-It state. However, the individual must attempt to transform the I-It into an I-Thou. For Buber, concern for the presence of God should be our unqualified primary interest.

Psycho-Halakhic Man of Conscience

Judaism is based on obedience to God. Through conscience, it is not God who is being heard, but the inner voice of man. The Jew, however, is required to listen to God's word.

What is conscience?

Does it refer to an autonomous view, whereby man recognizes in conscience what is right and what is wrong? This recognition does not consist of hearing an external judgment - i.e., the will of God - but is an internal act of recognizing the moral truth. Conscience is an affirmation of our sense of

23

right, very often in conflict with the judgment of society, with the religious structure and possibly even with God.

Thus, conscience is an affirmation of ethical humanism, of the moral self-sufficiency of man, who in the final analysis must make his own judgments. Professor Isaiah Leibowitz claims that conscience is an atheistic category in Judaic thought (Leibowitz, 1979, pp. 14-15). Leibowitz emphasizes the dichotomy between the Kantian autonomy of man and the Jewish teaching of heteronomy (Falk, 1981, p. 66).

If conscience is understood in this way, it is not easily reconcilable with an ethic that looks to the word of God as its criterion of what is right. The Divine word is the judge of man's moral sense.

Conscience, however, can also be understood as the voice of God speaking to man in solitude. Man is able to determine what is right in God's view, not in man's. Wyschogrod states: "In this heteronomous view of conscience, there is no fundamental difference between obedience to God when God directly addresses man and listening to the voice of conscience in which it is also the voice of God that is being heard" (Wyschogrod, 1981, p. 321).

However, differentiating between an autonomous conscience driven by ethical humanism, and an heteronomous conscience generated by listening to the inner voice of God addressing man, is really semantic meaninglessness. Both forms of conscience are the voice of another calling us to our responsibility, along with realization that the voice at the same time seems to be coming from within us. On this level, God (who demands) and man (of whom the demand is made) are a unified whole (Wyschogrod, 1981, p. 323).

Within this discussion, an ethic of conscience has the potential of drifting into a Godless proclamation of human independence. After all, cannot man rely on himself to discover the good - not only universally and abstractly, but also in the concreteness of the existential situation in which conscience makes itself heard in judging the right of specific instances? It must be remembered, however, that this autonomous direction of conscience exists solely in relation to the Divine word. Conscience points beyond itself to the good or right which is sensed by conscience but not created by it (Wyschogrod, 1981, pp. 323-325).

In Biblical theology, it is the Divine word that is at the center of attention. Must the believing Jew therefore sacrifice his conscience in obeying God? May man give up an

24

ultimate individuality when he embraces the covenant, knowing that the covenant has a more national character than an individual one? Is conscience the "Isaac" in each one of us, which we must be prepared to offer on the altar of Divine sacrifice?

What is the relationship of obedience to God to one's conscience? Is not the very act of obedience ultimately dependent on the dictate of one's innermost conscience? Thus, even the act of submission on the part of man is affirmed in the depth of one's conscience. This is indeed the essence of the doctrine of free will, which is so crucial in the development of the spiritual personality (Deuteronomy 30:15). A Jew who remains faithful to the covenant is acting out of conscience and not social conformity.

The covenantal Jew is ipso facto a man of conscience. What happens when conscience and law conflict? If conscience is the motivating force behind the covenantal Jew, it must also be followed when conscience and law contradict one another. "If conscience is to have any authority, it must have all authority" (Wsychogrod, 1981, p. 327). Conscience must be obeyed even when it contradicts the Divine law as it is objectively understood. The law, as understood objectively, must be obeyed as one hears it now in the depth of one's conscience. Eugene Borowitz similarly understands Wsychogrod's (1981) contention:

> that the individual conscience must be granted rights even when to us it appears to be acting in error. Not to do so would negate the very concept of conscience for a heteronomous revelation would have effectively usurped our God-given right to think and judge for ourselves. (Borowitz, 1984, p. 50)

The well known Talmudic dictum, "For Rabbi Hanina said, He who is commanded and fulfills the command, is greater than he who fulfills it though not commanded (Talmud, Kiddushin 31a)," seems to indicate a significant preference for an individual who obeys the commandment because it is commanded by God, rather than for someone who obeys commandments as a result of his conscience. However, Ephraim Urbach (1969) brilliantly interprets this comment contextually, as specifically referring to categories of people, such as non-Jews, women, and blind individuals which the Torah exempts from the performance of certain commandments or commandments in general (Talmud, Baba Kamma 38a, 87a; Abodah Zarah 3a). He specifically states that Rabbi Hanina was not emphasizing heteronomy over autonomy (Urbach, 1969, pp. 286-287).

25

The dialectic tension of autonomy and conscience within Judaism is succinctly expressed in the Hebrew word Mitzvah, which literally means commandment. However, with every Mitzvah there is a Divine law-giver, Mitzave, and a human law recipient, Mitzuve. The balance between all three of these elements highlights the significance of the role of conscience and autonomy within Judaism.

The opening line of the Code of Jewish law (Karo, Shulhan Arukh, Orach Hayyim) states: "A man should strengthen himself as a lion to get up in the morning to the service of his Creator." Rabbi Karo's beginning restates the outlook of Judah ben Tema, who suggested that a leonine resolve and other attributes are appropriate as one fulfills the will of God (Mishnah, Abot 5:23). Rabbi Karo, however, wrote an introduction to the Code of Jewish law that was printed only once - in the Venice edition in 1565. In this introduction, he explains the purposes of the Code of Jewish law. Its first purpose is that a Rabbinic scholar should have the law easily accessible; and secondly, that the uninitiated students can easily find a guide to daily behavior. Thus, one can understand that the phrase calling upon man to "strengthen himself as a lion" to serve God was directed primarily toward uninitiated students, who desired to be guided exclusively by the Halakhah. However, for the person who is guided also by Lifnim Mishurat Hadin and Imitatio Dei, in contrast to the uninitiated student, the goal is also to internalize the Halakhah and follow one's conscience when this is deemed appropriate.

Rabbi Karo eliminated ideology and theology from the text of the Shulhan Arukh. It contains no philosophical prolegomenon. Rabbi Karo was not concerned with ethical underpinning or theological vision of Halakhah. The omission of these trans-Halakhic materials created a picture of life which is characterized by regularity, routine, and stability. The absence of an ideational framework and a rationale of the law made it difficult for the Rabbinic scholar and the uninitiated student to utilize the Halakhic concepts of Lifnim Mishurat Hadin and Imitatio Dei concomitantly with the practice of the law. "If the Shulhan Arukh only charts a specific way of life but does not impart a specific version or vision of meta-Halakhah, it is because the latter is to be supplied and experienced independently" (Twersky, 1982, pp. 142-143, 147, and footnote 43).

In order to listen to conscience, it is one's responsibility to have a conscience in good working order. There must be a willingness to listen to conscience - not only to what we want to hear, but to what conscience is actually saying, however painful its message may be. Furthermore, conscience needs to be sensitized and developed by God's

26

revelation. God's revelation refers not only to the Torah but also to the more universal revelation of the history of mankind and the creation of the world (Maimonides, Yesodei HaTorah 2:1; Melakhim 11:4-uncensored version). Conscience does not necessarily mean acting autonomously. In order for conscience to be ethical it must be well developed. The development of an ethical conscience requires an elaborate process of education.

An autonomous conscience is differentiated from an heteronomous conscience. An autonomous conscience stems from one's inner voice. An heteronomous conscience is derived by a person's sense that one's inner voice is not a voice of solitude, but God addressing man.

The difficulty in ascertaining whether one's conscience is autonomous or heteronomous is that making such a determination is dependent on one's belief system; it is not a decision that can be verified empirically. It is not a situation in which the correspondence theory of truth is operational. This theory states that ideas and reality are in agreement with one another based on sense perception and our power of reason. The belief system that ultimately determines whether an autonomous or heteronomous conscience is functional is dependent on what is called a psychic truth.

Jung states a very basic and fundamental principle of psychology: physicality is not the only criterion of truth. There are also psychic truths. These psychic truths cannot be verified in any physical or empirical way.

Religious statements are in the category of psychic truths. They refer to things that cannot be established as physical facts. Psychic truths are independent of physical data. Religious statements are ultimately psychic confessions; such statements reflect our images of what is ineffable (Jung, 1973, pp. xi and xii). The Hymn of Glory similarly expresses, "They imaged Thee, not as Thou art really; they described Thee by Thy acts only" (Birnbaum, 1949, p. 418).

Religious psychic truths have an objective and subjective side. The objective side is the content of religious belief; and the subjective side is the form in which this content is given to man, and the attitude that man adopts toward the content. The subjective side represents a personal faith, one which cannot be proved to someone who does not believe in it. This religious belief is not based on scientific proofs; it is an immediate certainty. This certainty in the object of faith is utterly personal (Guttmann, 1976, p. 23-25).

27

Conscience, whether autonomous or heteronomous, is a psychic phenomenon. And even when conscience contradicts one's objective understanding of the Divine law, the decision to follow the law or one's conscience is ultimately a manifestation of one's psychic understanding of God's revelation.

In contrast, Spero (1985) hypothesizes that there are two ways to acknowledge the religious patient's feelings and beliefs related to God. One way is to acknowledge these feelings as an aspect of the patient's psychological reality; a second approach accepts these feelings as actual phenomena. Spero's hypothesis has no practical significance in this context since all of man's actions ensue from psychological reality or actual phenomena. As Jung asserted, all religious statements are psychic truths and not amenable to verifiability.

Psycho-Religious Man of Conscience

The psycho-Halakhic man of conscience in Judaism finds his parallel form in the psycho-religious man of conscience in Christianity. The dialetic between heteronomy and conscience was clearly expressed in the life of Tolstoy.

Tolstoy's "religious doctrine, accepted on trust and supported by external pressure, thaws away gradually under the influence of knowledge and experience of life which conflict with it, and a man very often lives on imagining that he still holds intact the religious doctrine imparted to him in childhood, whereas in fact not a trace of it remains" (Tolstoy, 1983, pp. 667-668). The experience of life is Tolstoy as a subject-conscience man, whereas the trust and pressure is Tolstoy as an object man.

Tolstoy, as a psycho-religious man of conscience, claimed that, "Therefore the arbiter of what is good and evil is not what people say and do, but it is my heart and I" (Tolstoy, 1983, p. 674). After he had regained his faith, Tolstoy still allowed his conscience to be operational. This further demonstrates that even his faith was ultimately based on conscience.

Tolstoy observed the rites of the Church -- though only those rites that his conscience allowed for. He frequently concealed from himself the contradictions and obscurities of theology, while not denying himself faith -- a faith that was necessary for him to find some meaning in an otherwise meaningless existence. Tolstoy stated:

During church service I attended to every word and gave them a meaning whenever I could. In the Mass the most important words for me were: "Let us love one another in conformity!" The further words, "In unity we believe in the Father, the Son, and Holy Ghost," I passed by, because I could not understand them. (Tolstoy, 1983, p. 720)

Tolstoy's decision to once again receive the Eucharist, after neglecting this rite for many years, was an act of conscience. The Communion was explained as an act performed in remembrance of Christ and indicating a purification from sin. Tolstoy was delighted that he was able to join the faith of his fathers and the milliards of country peasants. However, when he had to proclaim that what he was about to swallow was truly flesh and blood, his conscience exclaimed that this was false.

Tolstoy interjected subjective understanding into objective religious rites whenever possible. "However, when I forced an explanation into them, it made me feel that I was lying, thereby quite destroying my relation to God and depriving me of all possibility of belief" (Tolstoy, 1983, p. 721).

My personal issue in this area deals with the sacrificial prayers recited in the Sabbath and Holiday liturgy.

Do I believe in the restoration of animal sacrifice in the Temple? I am torn betwixt and between. The entire Book of Leviticus is primarily devoted to the laws of serving God via animal sacrifices. The Talmud devoted one-sixth of all its discussion to sacrifices. Today, I regularly recite the prayers relating to animal sacrifices. But what is in my heart and conscience as I say them? My conscience dictates that there is the possibility of the abrogation of certain laws in the future.

Some Midrashic utterances suggest the possibility of an abrogation of certain laws in the future world. Jewish mysticism allows for the Torah to be read in different ways throughout successive generations (Altmann, 1969, p. 112).

Thus, I have found some Rabbinic utterances that sanction my inner voice. And I am further comforted by knowing that this tension existed in Maimonides as well.

Maimonides states (Mishneh Torah, Melakhim 11:1) that in the time of the Messiah, sacrifices will be reinstated. In Maimondes' Guide of the Perplexed (3:32) he explains that the primary reason for the Bible's introduction of sacrifices was the nature of early man - i.e., the fact that he was accustomed

29

to offering up animals to pagan deities. Rather than attempting to change human nature, God allowed sacrifices to remain but transferred them to His own name.

Thus the nature of man was crucial in introducing the concept of sacrifice, and may be an equal factor in its eventual abrogation. My recitation of the sacrificial prayers is currently performed with ambivalence. This ambivalence represents another variation of the psycho-Halakhic man of conscience. I hesitate to abrogate the law, yet I (my conscience) struggles for its eventual legal abrogation.

Implications for a Study of

Psychology and Judaism

The study of psychology and Judaism is still in its infancy. Observations regarding the literature in psychology and Judaism have already been surveyed (Spero, 1980, 3-7). Dr. Reuven Bulka is to be credited for having started the Journal of Psychology and Judaism in 1976. This journal has provided a forum for a serious investigation of the relationship between psychology and Judaism.

The most significant study in this field has been the work of Moshe Spero, who maintains that Halakhah precedes human reality, in the form of an a priori theoretical structure. This a priori structure is the foundation of reality. This Halakhic reality determines an appropriate psychological reality for man. Through a Halakhic ontology, human behavior ensues. Spero diagrams this as follows:

Halakhic ontology model:

cross-cultural
expression of
such need

Given: Halakhic a priori
forms   psychological needs

Halakhic
expression

(Spero, 1980, pp. 14-30).

Spero's Halakhic a priori model presupposes specific human needs, and creates a means for fulfilling these human needs. The difficulty with Spero's approach is that, philosophically and psychologically, it views man exclusively as an object. The Torah's purpose, as derived from Lifnim Mishurat Hadin and

30

Imitatio Dei, is that its entire teachings, normative as well as homiletical, will create the psycho-<u>Halakhic</u> man of conscience, which includes man-as-subject as well.

Since Spero discusses grief and bereavement as part of the resolution of experiencing a death in the family, this will serve as my example as well. Spero maintains that this <u>Halakhic</u> <u>a priori</u> form makes grief and mourning a possibility and substantiates the development of cross-cultural expressions of bereavement (Spero, 1980, 22-23). Specifically, the Torah addresses the concrete <u>Halakhic</u> institutionalization of bereavement via the laws of mourning. "Cross-cultural expressions of bereavement, even though they may not manifest <u>Keriah</u> (rending one's garment) or other specific Jewish guidelines, retain this essential <u>Halakhic</u> nature" (Spero, 1980, p. 22). What is inherent in <u>Keriah</u> is inherent in the human psychology of bereavement. This can be diagrammed as:

cross-cultural
expressions of
guilt.

Given: <u>Halakhic</u> <u>a priori</u>
      <u>Aveilut</u>   need for catharsis
      (mourning)

<u>Keriah</u>,
(rending one's
garment).

Thus, a <u>Halakhic</u> <u>a priori</u> law is the blueprint of human nature.

But this <u>Halakhic</u> <u>a priori</u> model objectifies man, and does not allow for the subjective human experience. The psycho-<u>Halakhic</u> man of conscience incorporates the basic <u>Halakhic</u> guidelines of human behavior, and allows man to utilize these norms in a manner that will allow the subjective man to emerge as well. An example will clarify.

The Rabbis decreed that as part of the bereavement process, friends and relatives should comfort the mourner for seven days (Talmud, Moed Katan 19a). Spero's <u>Halakhic</u> <u>a priori</u> model, as well as Rabbi Soloveitchik's <u>Halakhic</u> man, perform this commandment in a thorough and meticulous fashion, incorporating all the minutiae and details of this delicate <u>mitzvah</u> (commandment).

The psycho-<u>Halakhic</u> man of conscience looks not only at the individual mourner during the seven-day period; he also realizes that the seven-day period is only the basic guideline in providing comfort. The psycho-<u>Halakhic</u> man of conscience

31

looks also at the bitter-cold, isolated eighth day of mourning for which no specific commandment exists to comfort the mourner - but where the commandments of Lifnim Mishurat Hadin and Imitatio Dei clearly delineate an entirely different way of approaching the seven-day period, that eighth day, and the entire year. The clear delineation of the various time-frames of mourning (seven days, 30 days, 12 months) sets guidelines not only for the mourner but also for the community, which must assist the mourner in gradually rejoining that community. It is this concept of conscience coupled with psychological sensitivity that creates the fusion of subject/object man of conscience, or the psycho-Halakhic man of conscience.

It is ironic that on occasion, a true understanding of indigenous Torah values can motivate one to violate a Halakhic norm. The Talmud (Berakhot 54a) interprets the verse "It is time to act for the Lord; they have made void your Torah" (Psalms 119:126), as allowing for the temporary abolition of Jewish law for the fortification of Judaism. The psycho-Halakhic man of conscience calls for a response to concrete situations that may differ from the objective Halakhah. This approach can begin an entirely new investigation of psychology and Judaism, one based not on a Halakhic a priori model but on a psycho-Halakhic conscience model.

The ideal that emerges, then, is that the human condition is one of contemplation and spirituality. On the other hand, Judaism requires man to act. In spite of the existing tension, one aspect cannot exist without the other; nearness to God obligates man to take moral action. Even the joy of basking in the reflection of the Divine splendor is conditional upon moral conduct, and may be achieved by virtue of such conduct. Judaism speaks of nearness to God: "Whom have I in heaven but Thee?, and besides Thee I desire none upon earth" (Psalms 73:25). Man yearns for proximity to God, and for distance from all things which hinder this proximity.

Only the personal God can be a commanding God. There are religious rituals whose observance is expressed by accepting the obligation to implement the precepts; and, on the other hand, there is prayer. There is content in prayer - man prays about something - but the essence of prayer is direct contact with God.

For the believer, religious truth is irrevocable. At the same time it is an individual truth, a personal faith. Notwithstanding the internal conviction it may arouse in the believer, it is in no way transferable. It is not empirically verifiable. Ultimately, its source is in the psyche.

A further illustration of the psyche and conscience which form an integral part of the psycho-<u>Halakhic</u> man of conscience can be seen in Maimonides' <u>Mishneh Torah</u>, which codifies the entire corpus of Jewish law. Despite the overall tone of "permitted" or "prohibited" evident throughout Maimonides' code, on various occasions Maimonides interjects the importance of value judgments. These statements are conceptually similar to Nahmanides' comment on, "You shall be holy" (Leviticus 19:2).

Isadore Twersky's (1980) analysis of Maimonides' <u>Mishneh Torah</u> also emphasizes the necessary fluidity within Jewish law. He states:

> For example: "if he does any of these things, he is, though fulfilling his duty, guilty of unbecoming conduct" (Maimonides, Mishneh Torah, Keriat Shema 2:8). Maimonides also condemns behavior which, while technically permissible, "incurs the displeasure of the Sages" (Maimonides, Mishneh Torah, Nahalot 6:11; Issure Biah 21:11). Some things may even be blameworthy even though not formally forbidden (Maimonides, Mishneh Torah, Nahalot 11:12). <u>Halakhah</u> urges the individual to act in such a way as to avoid arousing even the suspicion of wrongdoings. One's behavior should not only be legally unimpeachable, but also sensitive, noble, and thoughtful. These Maimonidean statements are particularly noteworthy, since they emanate from his code of Jewish law. Maimonides understood that even a precise code must leave room for elasticity. The precise directives are intermingled with an encouragement to achieve transcendent goals.
>
> Maimonides realizes that law has built-in uncertainties. A Rabbi or judge is always faced with unimagined new constructs. Although law tries to capture unpredictable reality, there is always the fluidity of each particular situation to be considered. Maimonides reminds the judge (Mishneh Torah, Yibbum 8:12,13) that you must always, in all these doubtful cases, take care to be guided by these fundamental principles... in this manner you must interpret and render decisions in all doubtful cases that may occur in matters touching levirate marriage... according as we have explained all the principles you are to rely upon (Mishneh Torah, Yibbum 8:12,13). The judge is given a creative-interpretive role in procedural as well as substantive matters. Judicial discretion and legal rigidity are incompatible. Discretionary power is vested in the

judge in this matter, as it is impossible to lay down detailed rules on this subject. (Mishneh Torah, Edut 9:10; Twersky, 1980, pp. 134-135)

The judge must be guided by his conscience, and this cannot be codified. Maimonides states:

> With regard to all these disciplinary measures, discretionary power is vested in the judge. He is to decide whether the emergency of the hour demands their application. But whatever the expedient he sees fit to resort to, all his deeds should be done for the sake of heaven. Let not human dignity be light in his eyes; for the respect due to man supersedes a negative Rabbinical command. (Mishneh Torah, Sanhedrin 24:10)

Thus Maimonides, the "Halakhic Man" par excellence, is cognizant of fluidity within law. He therefore requires wisdom, experience, creative interpretation, intuition, justice, and compassion in rendering decisions based on objective law. Halakhah and reality, the logic of law and the contingencies of life, must be aligned and reconciled. Halakhic man must be transformed to the Halakhic man of conscience. David Hartman (1985) sees the transformation as a central part of the living covenant. He states:

> Maimonides states that when philosophical opinion clashes with the literal meaning of the Bible, one must ascertain whether the philosophical assertion has been truly demonstrated. If it has not, then one accepts literally what the Bible says. If, on the other hand, the assertion has been demonstrated, Maimonides maintains that one is obliged to reinterpret the Bible figuratively. (Guide 2:25)

> For Maimonides, the Torah could not require us to sacrifice our human powers of reason. Similarly, the Torah never asks us to sacrifice our ability to judge what is fair and just. Our human ethical sense shapes our understanding of what is demanded of us in the mitzvot [commandments]. Our subjective powers of reason determine when those commandments are applicable, and when they are temporarily preempted by the more intrinsic morality of the Torah. That means that the development of the Halakhah must be subjected to the scrutiny of moral categories that are independent of the notion of Halakhic authority.

> Just as Maimonides utilized the human capacity to arrive at truth independent of revelation and Rabbinic authority, so too must our human ethical sense shape

34

our understanding of what is demanded of us in the
mitzvot. The human ethical sense, even when it has
sources of authority other than revelation or Rabbinic
interpretation, acts in response to and within a
relationship with God. Halakhic ethics are not acted
out in a spirit of human isolation; the point of
departure is always covenantal, and men always view
themselves as being in the presence of God. (Hartman,
1985, pp. 98-100)

Psycho-Halakhic Man of Conscience in American Law

The psycho-Halakhic man of conscience is similarly
reflected in the legal and philosophical system of American
law.

Fuller insists that law and morals should not be
distinguished. The legal process should also not be
differentiated from the results. He bases his theory on the
fact that law is intrinsically purposive and therefore value-
laden and moral. A law's meaning can only be ascertained by
knowing its purposes. When interpreting a law, we must
understand the value of the purposes (Fuller, 1969).
Therefore, every judge, in rendering a decision, refers to an
intrinsic aspect of law itself -- i.e., its moral component.

Second, Fuller argues that a system of legal rules also has
its own purpose. "Subjecting human conduct to the governance
of rules" goes beyond the specific purposes of that system's
individual precepts (Fuller, 1969, p. 105). To fulfill this
purpose, law must be sufficiently general, public, prospective,
clear and intelligible, free from contradiction, constrained
through time, possible to obey, and administered according to
its requirements. Law without these attributes ceases to be
law at all. These principles of legality are moral principles
and confer upon law an "internal morality," regardless of the
law's content. Similarly, legal process is intrinsically moral
in enabling disputing parties an equal opportunity to present
facts and arguments. The internal morality of civil
adjudication provides a connection between law and morals
(Fuller, 1969, p. 106).

Although Fuller was not a theological-natural lawyer who
believed that law or morals were authored by God, he espoused
many elements of the natural law tradition, including his
belief that law and morals should not be sharply distinguished.

Judges must refer to a law's intrinsically moral purpose in
order to ascertain its meaning and to apply it to specific
facts; these purposes are part of the legal system. Reference
to moral purpose is thus required by the rule of law.

35

Because law is intrinsically purposive, Fuller opposed teaching mere black-letter law. Legal education, he said, should examine underlying purposes, since they are the intrinsic constituents of law itself.

Law intrinsically possesses certain attributes that are moral - underlying purposes and built-in structural attributes that inherently affect morality.

By interpreting law in the context of its larger purposes, judges allow for the ambiguity of legal language, while applying a standard external to their own values. At the same time, the larger "purposes" underlying judges' decisions are part of law, not external to it; judges look within law, rather than beyond it, when they apply these purposes.

The "internal morality of law" is Fuller's way of describing the psycho-Halakhic man of conscience (Powers, 1985, pp. 221-235).

Conclusion

1) Conscience is an integral part of Jewish law and thought, as manifested in the Halakhic concepts of Imitatio Dei and Lifnim Mishurat Hadin.

2) The predominant view of the Halakhic man consists of man exclusively as an object. It lacks the emphasis of man's other component of man-as-subject. Rabbi Soloveitchik's Halakhic man shows his creative heroism by negating self, and becoming subservient to the will of God. The prototype of the religious Halakhic man is Abraham's submissiveness in accepting the Divine decree to sacrifice his son, Isaac.

3) Dr. Moshe HaLevi Spero's paradigm model of the integration of psychology and Judaism utilizes an a priori Halakhic model. This model also views man as an object, without allowing man's experience of the world to affect this a priori Halakhic model. Theoretically, this a priori Halakhic model rests on an intimate knowledge of man's nature, so that all his future human needs can be guided and channeled by a pre-determined construct. This model also does not include the unique nature of every man's subjectivity, and how he experiences the world as man-as-subject.

4) Martin Buber's view of the religious man is manifested in the I-Thou relationship. In the I-Thou relationship, man-as-subject is aware of the presence of God. This model does not offer any normative guidelines to direct man in any Halakhic fashion. Man-as-object is totally subsumed in an I-It relationship, where man is removed from the presence of God.

36

In this model, the Torah, as an expression of Divine revelation, guides man by Divine legislation, and obfuscates man's yearning for unity with the Shekhinah (Divine Presence). This model does not include the essential Mitzvah (commandment).

5) The concept of psycho-Halakhic man allows man-as-subject to co-exist with man-as-object. This adds a dimension to Soloveitchik's and Spero's models. This new model allows for a fusion of a subject/object modality, in which man's subjective experience of his world is united with Divine objective law in creating a man of synthesis -- man as an object and man as a subject. Similarly, this model adds to Buber's model the necessity of an objective Divine legal system.

6) The psycho-Halakhic man must be able to fuse this subject/object dichotomy based on his conscience. The element of conscience must attempt to understand the inner morality of the law at the present moment, in specific circumstances. Man's conscience must serve as a check-and-balance system in the fusion of man's subject/object elements. The psycho-Halakhic man of conscience is not submissive when such subservience runs contrary to his autonomous sense of ethics and morality. Neither does the psycho-Halakhic man of conscience follow dictates of situational ethics. The psycho-Halakhic man of conscience utilizes the objective Halakhic guidelines, and grapples with understanding the inner morality and ethics of that law. He experiences the presence of God even as he integrates the here-and-now. Man's conscience reconciles the object/subject dichotomy, allowing man to hear and experience the living God talking to him. In that way, the quintessential aspects of the Torah, Imitatio Dei and Lifnim Mishurat Hadin are fully implemented. This approach places the psycho-Halakhic man of conscience in a constant dynamic balance, in contrast to a static balance. As Alfred North Whitehead proclaimed, there is change in the midst of order, and order in the midst of change (Whitehead, 1929). It is this model that can be used to delineate a new approach to psychology and its relationship to Judaism.

37

Postscript

Adolf Hitler told Hermann Rauschning, president of the Danzig Senate: "I liberated men from the filthy, humiliating, poisonous folly called conscience and morals" (Knight, 1969, p. 139).

This introductory work has accentuated the central role of conscience in Judaism.

References

Altmann, A. (Ed.). (1969). "Saadya Gaon" <u>Three Jewish Philosophers</u>. New York: Atheneum.

Belkin, S. (1978). <u>The Philosophy of Purpose</u>. New York: Yeshiva University Press.

Berman, S. (1977, 1975). "Lifnim Mishurat Hadin," <u>Journal of Jewish Studies</u>. Volume 26, pp. 86-104; Volume 28, pp. 181-193.

Birnbaum, P. (1949). <u>Daily Prayer Book</u>. New York: Hebrew Publishing Company.

Blidstein, G. (1975). <u>Honor thy Father and Mother</u>. New York: Ktav Publishing.

Borowitz, E.B. (1984). "The Autonomous Jewish Self," <u>Modern Judaism</u>. Volume 4, Number 1, Feb., pp. 39-57.

Buber, M. (1967). <u>On Judaism</u>. New York: Schocken Books.

<u>Encyclopaedia Judaica</u>. (1971). Jerusalem: The MacMillan Company.

<u>Encyclopedia of Religion & Ethics</u>. (1952). Edinburgh: T.& T. Clark. Originally published 1926.

Falk, Z.W. (1981). <u>Law & Religion</u>. The Jewish Experience. Mesharim Publishers: Jerusalem.

Fox M. (1979). "The Philosophical Foundations of Jewish Ethics: Some Initial Reflections," <u>The Second Annual Rabbi Louis Feinberg Memorial Lecture in Judaic Studies</u>. Cincinnati: University of Cincinnati.

Fuller, L.L. (1969). <u>The Morality of Law</u>. Revised Edition. Yale University Press: New Haven.

Guttmann, J. (1955). <u>Religion & Knowledge</u>. (Hebrew). Bergman, S.H., and Rotenstreich, N. (Eds.). Jerusalem: Magnes Press, The Hebrew University.

Guttmann, J. (1976). <u>On the Philosophy of Religion</u>. Jerusalem: Magnes Press, The Hebrew University.

Hartman, D. (1985). <u>A Living Covenant</u>: The Innovative Spirit in Traditional Judaism. Free Press: New York.

Heineman, I. (1954). <u>Darchei Haagadah</u>. Jerusalem: Hebrew University Press.

Heller, A. L. (18th Century). <u>Kezot ha-Hoshen</u>. (1960). Jerusalem: Pardes.

Hirsch, S.R. (1978). <u>The Hirsch Siddur</u>. New York: Feldheim Publishers.

<u>The Holy Scriptures</u> (3 Vols.) (1982). Philadelphia: Jewish Publication Society.

Jung, C.G. (1973). <u>Answer to Job</u>. Princeton: Princeton University Press. Originally published 1960.

Kaufman, W.E. (1976). <u>Contemporary Jewish Philosophies</u>. New York: Reconstructionist Press and Behrman House.

Karo, J. (16th Century). <u>Shulhan Arukh</u> (10 Vols). 1965. New York: M.P.Press.

Kierkegaard, S. (1941). Concluding Unscientific Postcript. Princeton University Press: Princeton.

Knight, J.A. (1969). Conscience and Guilt . New York: Appleton-Century-Crofts, Meredith.

Laing, R.D. (1967). The Politics of Experience. New York: Pantheon.

Landman, L. (1969). "Law and Conscience: The Jewish View," Judaism. Volume 18, Number 1, Winter, pp. 17-30.

Leeuw, G.v.d. (1938). Religion in Essence and Manifestation. New York: Harper. Originally published 1933.

Leibowitz, I. (1979). Yahadut, Am Yehudi, Umedinat Yisrael. (Hebrew). Jerusalem: Schocken Books.

Lichtenstein, A. (1975). "Does Jewish Tradition Recognize an Ethic Independent of Halakha?" Modern Jewish Ethics. Fox, M. (Editor). Ohio: Ohio State University Press.

Linzer, N. (1984). The Jewish Family: Authority and Tradition in Modern Perspective . Human Sciences Press: New York.

The Midrash (10 Vols.) (1961). H.Freedman and M. Simons (Eds.). London: Soncino Press.

Maimonides, M. (12th Century) (1962). Mishneh Torah. (6 Vols.) New York: M.P. Press.

Maimonides, M. (12th Century) (1963). The Guide of the Perplexed. S. Pines (translator). Chicago: The University of Chicago Press.

Nahmanides Commentary on the Torah (13th Century) (1975). Charles Chavel (Translator). New York: Shilo Publishing House.

Peck, S. (1979). The Road Less Traveled. New York: Touchstone Books. Simon and Schuster.

Powers, Jr., W. (1985). Book Review. L.L. Fuller by Robert Summers in Duke Law Journal. Volume 1985.

Poole, R. (1972). Towards Deep Subjectivity. New York: Harper and Row.

Random House Dictionary of the English Language. (1967). J. Stein (Ed.). New York: Random House

Sartre, J.P.(1956). Being and Nothingness. New York: Philosophical Library.

Scholem. G. G. (1965). On the Kabbalah and Its Symbolism. New York: Schocken Books.

Shilo, S. (1978). "On One Aspect of Law and Morals in Jewish Law: Lifnim Mishurat Hadin," Israel Law Review. Volume 13, pp. 359-390.

Sifra. In Malbim, M. (19th Century). Commentary to The Pentateuch: Leviticus (1964). New York: Grossman.

Soloveitchik, J.B. (1983). Halakhic Man. Translated by Lawrence Kaplan. Philadelphia: Jewish Publication Society. Originally published 1944.

Spero, M.H. (1980). Judaism and Psychology: Halakhic Perspectives. New York: Ktav Publishing House and Yeshiva University Press.

Spero, M.H. (1985). "The Reality and the Image of God in Psychotherapy," American Journal of Psychotherapy. Volume XXXIX, number 1, Jan., pp. 75-85.

Spero, S. (1983). Morality, Halakhah and the Jewish Tradition. New York: Ktav Publishing House and Yeshiva University Press.

The Talmud (19 Vols.) (1961). I. Epstein (Ed.). London: Soncino Press.

Tolstoy, L.N. (1983). "A Confession," The Portable Tolstoy. J. Bayley (Ed.). New York: Penguin Books.

Twersky, I. (1972). A Maimonides Reader. New York: Behrman House, Inc.

Twersky, I. (1980). Introduction to the Code of Maimonides (Mishneh Torah). Yale Judaica Series, Vol. XXII. New Haven & London: Yale University Press.

Twersky, I. (1982). "The Shulhan Arukh: Enduring Code of Jewish Law," Studies in Jewish Law and Philosophy. New York: Ktav Publishing House, pp. 130-148. Reprinted from Judaism, Volume XVI (1967), pp. 141-158.

Urbach, E.E. (1969). The Sages: Their Concepts and Beliefs. (Hebrew). Jerusalem: Magnes Press, The Hebrew University.

Whitehead, A. N. (1978). Process & Reality. Revised Edition. New York: Free Press. Originally published 1929.

Wyschogrod, M. (1981). "Judaism and Conscience," Standing Before God. Finkel, A., and Frizzell, L. (Eds.). New York: Ktav Publishing House.

PART II

On Integration

CHAPTER 2

Reflections on a Spiritual Dream

I was eagerly anticipating celebrating a quiet and meaningful Shavuot holiday with my wife, Marcie; our four children, Chana, Yosef Asher, Malka Mindel, and Yitzchak Shlomo; and my mother, who was visiting from New York.

The Mishnah and Targum Onkelos (Moed Katan 3:6; Numbers 28:26) refer to the holiday of Shavuot as Atzeret, meaning "conclusion." Just as Shmini Atzeret is the conclusion of the holiday of Sukkot, so too, Shavuot occurs seven weeks after Pesach and serves as the conclusion of Pesach. The redemption from physical slavery (i.e., Pesach) served as a precursor to the spiritual redemption which was made possible by the receipt of the Torah by the Israelites on the holiday of Shavuot.

My thoughts were focused on being able to rest--physically, mentally, and emotionally during the holiday. As Chaplain of Cedars-Sinai and as a psychotherapist, I have been and continue to be involved in many critical situations involving terminally ill cancer patients and clients with many varied psychotherapeutic issues. I was determined to allow myself to enjoy the holiday, barring emergencies.

After a joyous and festive family meal that evening, Marcie, Chana, Yosef Asher, and I gathered together to study the "Ten Commandments." We finished learning together, and Chana and Yosef Asher continued to study for several more hours. I felt very proud that our children independently chose to honor the tradition and custom of Torah study on the first night of Shavuot. They felt the excitement of the historical reenactment of the Divine Revelation of the Torah.

The next morning, we attended Shavuot services at our synagogue. The central aspect of the Shavuot services was the public reading of the "Ten Commandments" from the Torah. The entire congregation rose to listen to the Divine Revelation. The assembled congregants individually felt directly addressed by God and part of a collective as well. The collective consisted not only of those who were present in synagogues on that Holiday; there was a sense of being part of a larger collective dating back to our patriarch Abraham through the Biblical Moses to the medieval Moses Maimonides, up to the martyrs of the Holocaust and the war heroes of the State of Israel. This experience was a reaffirmation of our faith and a continuing link to the future generations of the Jewish people. By attending synagogue with my mother, wife and children, we establish the link of tradition from one generation to the next.

44

Shortly after we returned home and began our <u>Yom</u> <u>Tov</u> meal, my beeper went off and I called the hospital. The daughter of a terminally ill cancer patient asked me to visit and talk to her father because death was thought to be imminent. She said that he was a hospice patient in room 4114 and that he might not be alive the following day. I decided not to finish my <u>Yom</u> <u>Tov</u> meal, but rather to walk to the hospital, approximately 1 1/2 miles away. My daughter, Chana, sensing the long and lonely walk ahead, offered to walk with me and I accepted this altruistic offer. Being together shortened the walk and helped diminish the anxiety about what lay ahead.

Chana waited in the 4th floor lobby while I visited the patient, Mr. Isaac. As I entered the room, I immediately noticed that three generations of people were gathered. On each side of the patient's bed, his two grandsons were holding their grandfather's hand. The patient's wife was sitting in a chair adjacent to the bed, and his son and daughter were also seated in the room. I sensed the gravity of the moment in the room of this family-centered, dying patient. The patient was sitting up in his bed. The bright blue eyes of this 79-year-old, observant Polish Jew, Mr. Isaac, were strikingly distinguishable from his otherwise frail and emaciated appearance.

After exchanging <u>Yom</u> <u>Tov</u> greetings, I introduced myself to the patient. Our conversation took place in English and Hebrew. After a short while, the patient asked me to recite <u>Viduy</u> (confession) with him. As I was about to begin, he looked directly into my eyes and said, "Do you believe in <u>Viduy</u>?" Before I had a chance to respond, his daughter entered the dialogue. "But Dad," she said, "Mom was always the skeptic. You always showed uncompromising loyalty to the Jewish tradition." Continuing my talk with the patient and at the same time addressing his daughter's comments, I answered his question with a question. I asked him, "Do <u>you</u> believe in the recitation of <u>Viduy</u>?"

At that particular moment, I was aware of an uncomfortable feeling within me. My awareness was focused on desiring to be authentic and honest at a critical moment with a dying patient. What would be my response as a chaplain and what would be my response as a psychotherapist? Regardless of my professional orientation, what would be <u>my</u> orientation?

After some quiet reflection, the patient responded, "I have some doubts." Reaching out for his hand, I proclaimed that I shared his doubts as well. The patient reacted with a sigh of relief knowing that one can recite <u>Viduy</u> with faith and doubt. Doubt was not only sanctioned, it became an essential of the faith experience. We shared these philosophical thoughts. He then closed his eyes and together we recited the <u>Viduy</u> and

45

<u>Shema</u> - the prayer that represents the acceptance of the yoke of heaven and the reaffirmation of the Jew's faith.

I left Mr. Isaac, hoping I had helped him meet his ultimate challenge. Yet, there was another doubt within me. Why was my response so Rogerian and therapeutic? Perhaps I "should" have proclaimed, undauntedly and sincerely, "Yes, I do believe in the recitation of <u>Viduy</u>."

I left the patient's room saying, "Good <u>Yom Tov</u>, and I hope to see you tomorrow." He responded, "Good <u>Yom Tov</u>," with a bright smile on his face.

That night, I had the following dream regarding two <u>other</u> families, the Joseph and the Solomon family:

> I met Mrs. Joseph and her two adult step-daughters walking in the fifth-floor corridor at Cedars-Sinai Medical Center. I was quite puzzled at seeing this family together at this time. Mr. Joseph had recently died from leukemia, and during his prolonged illness and infrequent remissions, Mrs. Joseph and her two adult step-daughters always had differing views on how best to care for her husband and their father. Mr. Joseph's death only alienated the "family" even further. After exchanging brief greetings, I asked them if I could be of any assistance. They responded that they were looking for room 5905. [The female Russian immigrant who had taken care of their father suddenly had become seriously ill.]
>
> I silently hoped that their reference to room 5905 was a mistake, because that is where medical oncology was located--a room where dying patients generally choose not to receive comprehensive <u>hospice</u> care. Why didn't the hospital put her in the hospice unit in room 4122? I knew this room was empty due to the recent death of another patient, Mr. Solomon, with whom I had developed a long and loving relationship.
>
> While I am talking with the women, I see in the dream the following words from the Torah: "And I will take away my hand and you shall see my back; but my face shall not be seen." In the dream I realize that this sentence is an association with the fact that each time I entered room 4122, I first saw Mr. Solomon's back.

End of Dream

46

A brief explanation about my relationships with these two patients (in the dream) and their families is necessary before the interpretation.

The Joseph Family

Mr. Joseph, the terminally ill cancer patient in the dream, represents no doubt Mr. Isaac, the actual patient I saw the day before. My relationship with Mr. Joseph was characterized by rabbinic counseling as opposed to psychotherapy. My relationship with his wife was just the reverse. These differing relationships were reflective of our defined role and interaction with one another. Although undoubtedly my roles as rabbinic counselor and psychotherapist overlapped at times, these specialized roles were nevertheless maintained.

Working with them, both individually and as a couple, I felt bifurcated. In spite of my frustration with this process, their needs as individuals were being fulfilled for the moment. However, I did not feel unified and sensed the continuing need of integrating the roles of being a rabbi and a therapist.

The Solomon Family

My relationship with Mr. Solomon was very different. Mr. Solomon of room 4122 represented a patient (Erwin Altman - see Chapter 9, the epilogue) who had occupied room 4122 for a considerable time and who had passed away a few weeks before this dream. He was an outstanding personality, a man with whom I had many deep and spiritual discussions and to whom (as well as to members of his family) I had become very close. They encouraged the unification of my roles as a rabbi and as a psychotherapist. I became very close to Mr. Solomon and had given him a tribute several months before his death. In it I awarded him the deserved title of Morenu (our revered teacher). I was just then, at the time of the dream, in the process of preparing the publication of a brochure on this award-ceremony entitled:

M O R E N U
OUR REVERED TEACHER, GUIDE, AND COUNSELOR
A Singular Award-Ceremony
And
Tribute
to an
Outstanding Personality
Erwin Altman, J.D.

In the preface of this brochure his personality is described.

He was a shining example for us. With his deep uplifting

47

philosophy and love of life, he maintained his hope throughout, and supported it by his indomitable will and spirit. He chose to retain his conscious, creative, mental and spiritual faculties rather than let the great agonies of pain and suffering of cancer control the quality of his life. He was able to transform this reality to a higher spiritual dimension by his Messianic outlook and faith in Eternal Life. Even during the very last phase of his life, God granted him his wish; he rallied and, fully himself, was clearly communicating messages of love and prayers. (Meier, 1986, p. 6)

These messages of love and prayers concluded with Viduy, Shema, and the affirmations of faith (like at the close of the Day of ATONEMENT), which - in his own interpretation - express man's ultimate inner goal of AT-ONEMENT with his Higher SELF emanating from and eternally linked with the DIVINE UNFATHOMABLE ETERNAL REALITY.

Interpretation

The two patients in the dream, the Joseph family and Mr. Solomon, represented two distinct modes or stages of relating religion and psychology. The Joseph family represented the dis-ease of the split between religion and psychology; indeed, it accentuated the dichotomy of man's eternal yearning and quest for ultimate truth with his contrary subjective experience of life. Mr. Solomon, on the other hand, accentuated the ascension on Jacob's, (our Patriarch's) ladder. Mr. Solomon highlighted the tremendous possibilities afforded to man in his search for the ultimate and harmonious meanings of life. Mr. Solomon signified the stage which exists beyond the conflict of psychology and religion.

As one ascends the ladder of the harmonious relationship between psychology and religion, the gap between the finite human being and the Infinite Being becomes even more apparent. Mr. Solomon's back was always visible as I entered the room. Moses, the master of all prophets, was only privileged to see God's back. The ultimate secret and mystery of life was not even shown to Moses or King Solomon. Man is created in the Image of God; but only the "back" of the Image can be understood. The front of that Image, the face of God, is eclipsed for mankind eternally.

Mr. Solomon's room represented a lifelong, honest, intellectual and spiritual quest and exploration of life, illness, aging, death, and Messianic perspectives. He emanated the refreshing spirit of ongoing, dynamic inner

48

growth, during which the inner dialectic with doubt has been a stimulating friend towards integration on ascending levels. At the same time he realized that the mysteries on the highest levels of Jacob's "Ladder of Ascension" remain hidden from the human dimension, as the quantum leap between the finite human being and the infinite Divinity remain a mystery.

Implications of the Role of Doubt in Religious Development

Despite the eternal enigma which life presents, or perhaps, because of it--man throughout history has searched and explored the known and unknown in his quest to live in the Divine presence eternally. Man, who is created in God's image, struggles to understand himself, God, and the interrelationship of God and Man.

When Mr. Isaac asked me, "Do you believe in Viduy," why was I unable to respond with an affirmative yes? Furthermore, if I were a patient in that situation and I asked the same question of another chaplain, what response would serve me best?

The response that I gave to Mr. Isaac was client-centered. It allowed Mr. Isaac the opportunity to amplify on his question and doubt. My response to Mr. Isaac also reflected the core of my authentic feelings of sharing doubt and faith. Those two psychological insights represented my religious response at that moment.

This experience evoked in me once again that keen sense of spiritual loneliness that I feel within the Jewish community. The Jewish community, the rabbinical seminaries, the religious teachers and leaders generally do not allow for the peaceful coexistence of faith and doubt. In spite of the "official" position, the coexistence of faith and doubt is a reality which patients experience and which many great philosophers share as well.

Emanuel Rackman states that religious doubt ultimately refines faith. Doubt fosters humility and precludes fanaticism. He states:

Perhaps, like Socrates, I corrupt youth but I do teach that Judaism encourages questioning even as it enjoins faith and commitment. A Jew dare not live with absolute certainty, not only because certainty is the hallmark of the fanatic and Judaism abhors fanaticism, but also because doubt is good for the human soul, its humility, and consequently its greater potential ultimately to discover its Creator. (1970, p. 17)

49

In contrast, Norman Lamm has written an article entitled Faith and Doubt. Lamm concludes:

> We found that there is place for doubt within the confines of cognitive faith; it must not be allowed to interfere with normative halakhic practice, which is the expression of functional faith; and in affective faith we found that cognitive-type doubts can be met by creating a situation in which belief-that reverts to belief-in. (1971, p.30)

Having granted legitimacy to doubt, he limits this doubt to cognitive faith, and asserts that it must not affect functional faith or Halakhic practice. Furthermore, he states that "halakhah precedes and remains unconditioned by theology" (1971, p. 20). He does not exclude the possibility of doubt, but its admissability. The cognitive doubt must not disturb one's personal trust in God; it may reflect about God, but should not affect the I-Thou relationship with God.

Lamm's thesis is a factor in the genesis of contemporary man's spiritual loneliness within the Jewish community. His thesis leads to the dichotomy between psychology and religion, as the human quest for ultimate understanding has to disregard the intruding shadows of doubt. This troubles and stifles the approach to man's quest and this is represented by the Joseph family. But if doubt is integrated in the quest and psychology allowed as a tool for clarification, the limitations of psychology are recognized in the dynamic spiritual progress, and the dimension of faith reaches a stage beyond the concept of "conflict." This approach is represented by Mr. Solomon.

Mr. Solomon sanctions the totality of human experiences within an ongoing religious individual development. The covenant between man and God and the covenant between mankind and God becomes a living covenant.

Lamm effectively posits the legitimacy of cognitive doubt, carefully explaining that this should not interfere with either functional or affective faith. What is just as important, however, is the positive value of doubt in one's religious development. When doubt is confined only to a cognitive area, the religious man is transformed into a bifurcated religious man. He becomes the paradigmatic example of the Cartesian dualism of mind and body. Halakhic practices and trust in God become perfunctory at best. The Prophets bemoaned and lamented the performance of religious rituals devoid of an awareness of a living God (Isaiah 1:11). However, thinking and emotions are

50

constantly interwoven. Witness Job's reaction and his intense
rage when he curses the day he was born (Job 2:14).

Zvi Kurzweil (1985) also claims that the Bible has already
legitimized doubt in the area that Lamm calls affective faith.
He states:

> To come back to Lamm's categorization of faith and
> doubt: What he calls "affective" faith springs from
> love of God, trust and reliance in Him, and the
> category of doubt corresponding to this type of faith
> is already legitimized in the Bible because it is a
> concomitant of man's relation to God. It may even be
> argued that the closer and more intimate this
> relationship, the more intensive the human reaction to
> the injustices, cruelties, and catastrophes
> experienced in a world controlled by Divine
> Providence. We find Abraham arguing with God and
> asking Him rather reproachfully, "Wilt Thou consume
> the righteous with the wicked?" (Genesis 18:23).
> (1985, p. 76)

Tillich goes even further and states that doubt is struc-
turally anchored in religious faith. He states:

> If faith is understood as belief that something is
> true, doubt is incompatible with the act of faith. If
> faith is understood as being ultimately concerned,
> doubt is a necessary element in it. (1957, p. 18)
> Existential doubt and faith are poles of the same
> reality, the state of ultimate concern. (1957, p. 22)
> ...members of religious groups feel anxiety, guilt and
> despair about what they call "loss of faith." But
> serious doubt is confirmation of faith. (1957, p. 22)

Tillich acknowledges that doubt is a necessary element in
the dynamics of faith. Doubt, the uncertainty in faith, confirms man's process in the dynamics of faith. Doubt represents
the seriousness of the ultimate concern. Doubt is not considered as a negation of faith, but as an element which was always
and will always be present in the act of faith.

Doubt also contains a positive value in man's constant
religious search. Doubt awakens, and rekindles a new dialogue
with God. God can once again become a living reality. Just as
man develops biologically, psychologically, and socially
throughout his lifetime, it would be inaccurate to assume that
maturation does not take place religiously as well.

Some of the tenets and beliefs which were accepted and
understood in early adulthood may undergo refinement, modifica-

tion, and clarification. This development allows for an honest and authentic exploration in the integration of psychology and religion.

Mr. Isaac's doubt, as expressed by his question, "Do you believe in Viduy," represents his quest in reaching for God's hand as he was preparing to meet the Creator. In Mr. Isaac's transition from life to eternal life he was still experiencing religious growth.

I will remember Shavuot 5746 as a beautiful experience of spiritual growth.

References

Meier, L. (Ed.) (1986). "Morenu" Our Revered Teacher, Guide, and Counselor. A Singular Award-Ceremony and Tribute to an Outstanding Personality, Erwin Altman, J.D. Los Angeles: Cedars-Sinai Medical Center.

Kurzweil, Z. (1985). The Modern Impulse of Traditional Judaism. New Jersey: Ktav Publishing House.

Lamm, N. (1971). Faith and Doubt. New York: Ktav Publishing House; previously appeared in Tradition, volume 9, issue 1-2, 1967.

Rackman, E. (1970). One Man's Judaism. New York: Philosophical Library.

Tillich, P. (1957). Dynamics of Faith. New York: Harper and Row.

CHAPTER 3

A Modern Jew in Search of a Soul

GOD, Man and Halakhah (Jewish Law)

Jewish law is paradoxical but not contradictory in nature.
The nature of the paradox is that God, the law-giver, has given
His divine law to man, who grapples to understand the divine
law using his human faculty and capacity (Heller, 5720). This
union of divinity and humanity represents both the goal of the
divine plan as well as an eternal struggle between different
forces which encounter one another. This co-existence of
opposite and different forces exists both in man and in God.
The Torah describes man as a finite being. Man is finite
because he consists of two primary elements which represent man
qua man. Man is God's spirit and human flesh (Genesis 6:3).
Despite possessing God's spirit, man - precisely because of his
uniqueness and quality - cannot live forever. God, also, has
opposite and diametrically opposed characteristics which
describe the Almighty Himself. God is described as "He who
creates peace and evil" (Isaiah 45:7).

It is understandable that Jewish law and tradition, that
link which relates the divine will to man, would contain the
perplexing combination of divinity - humanity since each sphere
in and of itself combines diverse and paradoxical motives. As
previously explained, God has manifestations of peace and evil,
and humanity has both a divine spirit and human flesh. This
analysis can be graphically described as:

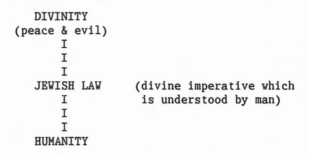

DIVINITY
(peace & evil)
I
I
I
JEWISH LAW   (divine imperative which
I   is understood by man)
I
I
HUMANITY

(divine spirit and human flesh)

How does man function in a universe which is composed of
dialectics? Does he sway like a pendulum from one extreme to
another until he achieves balance? More specifically, how does
man accept the "rule of the Kingdom of heaven" when there is a
perpetual struggle between God's spirit and human flesh?

54

Should the flesh be sublimated constantly to the spirit? Is integration and wholeness sacrificed forever?

The antithetical nature of reality is seen as well in abstract reality. Positive numbers co-exist with negative numbers; the laws of physics also demonstrate this principle.

Halakhah recognizes the duality of man's reality of spirit and flesh. Halakhah allows for the expression of both forces. The expression of both the divine spirit and the flesh is directed to God. Every commandment, either positive or negative, requires Kavannah - directional devoutness and piety to God. In contrast to secular legal systems which emphasize the implementation of a behavior, Jewish law accentuates behavior combined with inner feeling, piety and the devoutness of the person. Even when flesh has its fulfillment through food, sex, dance or companionship, it is all God-directed.

Halakhah's recognition of man's duality does not alleviate the struggle between man's flesh and spirit. This challenge faces the existential man and creates meaning for him.

The Nature of Religion

Within the framework of man's duality and dialectic, theologians and scholars have always distinguished between religion in essence and religion in manifestation (Leeuw, 1933).

Twersky (1974) stated that "the dialectical relationship between religion in essence and religion in manifestation is at the core of the Jewish religious consciousness" (p. 69). Halakhah, Jewish law, is the manifestation and concentration of a spiritual essence. Halakhah includes laws, religious institutions, and normative actions, while spirituality refers to moods, images, individual perceptions, and internal sensibilities. Manifestations and laws sometimes drift apart from essence and spirituality because a carefully constructed normative system cannot reflect fluid, spontaneous spiritual forces and motives.

Similar to Twersky (1974) but more universal in nature is Leeuw's (1933) thesis that religion consists primarily of essence and manifestations. He stated that reflection on the causes of natural phenomena cannot of itself constitute religion. It requires that the "object and subject are in a reciprocal operation." Man tries to elevate life, to enhance its value, to gain for it some deeper and wider meaning.

55

This balance between essence and manifestations has not always been maintained. James (1902) and Otto (1923) stressed the experimental aspects of religion, while Soloveitchik (1944) emphasized the implementation of the divine Law as the highest form of religious service.

James (1902) distinguished between institutional and personal religion. Institutional religion includes theology, ritual ceremonies, and ecclesiastical organizations. Personal religion refers to man's inner dispositions, his conscience, his feeling of helplessness, and the heart-to-heart, soul-to-soul relationship between man and his Maker. Religion cannot stand for any single principle -- it is a collective name for religious fear, love, awe, joy, and other elements. James defined religion as "feelings, acts, and experiences of individual men in their solitude, so far as they apprehend themselves to stand in relation to whoever they may consider the divine" (p. 31). The common man's perception of religion refers to a serious state of mind. However, James focused on man's total reaction to life. The concern of religion is with the manner of our acceptance of the universe. Religion makes easy what in any case is necessary, i.e., dependency on sheer mercy.

The supreme good is when we harmoniously adjust ourselves to unseen order. Within the religious sphere, articulated explanations are cogent only when they confirm pre-existing feelings and beliefs.

For some, the religion of healthy-mindedness leads to serenity, moral poise, and happiness. Feeling is a deeper source of religion than philosophic or theologic statements, which are secondary products. A "science of religion presupposes immediate experiences as their subject matter. Philosophy only corroborates our pre-existent partialities" (James, 1902, p. 424).

Otto (1923) likewise accentuated the essence of religion by emphasizing its numinous and other nonrational aspects. He stated that since expositions of religious truth are in language, these statements inevitably tend to stress the rational attributes of God. Otto (1923) stressed the concept of numinous -- the aspect of deity which transcends comprehension in rational or ethical terms. The rational and moral is an essential part of what we mean by holy or sacred, only it is not the whole of it; it includes nonrational elements as well. The holy, as a religious concept, is ineffable and it eludes definition. The numinous also involves a feeling of total dependence. This is an emotion of a creature that is overwhelmed by its own nothingness. This numinous feeling leads one to a vision of God as a _mysterium tremendum_. This view is similar to the religious view of

56

primitive man. Primitive man viewed God with dread, as an awful, majestic presence and therefore God was totally unapproachable. Man is conscious of a 'wholly other' that evades precise formulation in words. This nonrational aspect, in contrast to insight, is awakened by impulse, instinct, and the obscure forces of the subconscious.

In contrast to James (1902) and Otto (1923), Soloveitchik (1944) viewed the spiritual and religious person as synonymous with the man of the law. Every lifetime reality the Halakhic man approaches in an a priori fashion. For example, the setting of the sun signals the time for evening prayers, and the birth of children is seen as a fulfillment of the commandment of procreation. A few anecdotes amplify this position. As a child, Joseph Soloveitchik was once reading the Psalms on the High Holidays as an expression of piety. His father approached him and replaced his son's Book of Psalms with a book of Jewish laws on the High Holidays, saying "the service of God is identical with the study of Jewish law" (Soloveitchik, 1944, p. 706). In another Soloveitchik anecdote, a person in charge of blowing the ram's horn (Shofar) once began to show tears before the performance of this commandment. He was approached and told to restrain his emotions while he was performing the divine will. Soloveitchik is the prime exponent of the behavioristic, rational, and legalistic approach towards religion.

Religious Practice

This theoretical framework has been manifested on a practical level as well. Allport (1966) distinguished between an extrinsic and an intrinsic religious orientation. An extrinsic orientation means that religious devotion is not a value in its own right, but is an instrumental value serving the motives of person, comfort, security, or social status (Allport, 1966, p. 6). Examples of this approach are reflected in: "What religion offers me most is comfort when sorrows and misfortune strike," and "one reason for my being a church member is that such membership helps to establish a person in the community" (Allport, 1966, p. 6).

In contrast, intrinsic orientation "regards faith as a supreme value in its own right" (Allport, 1966, p. 6). Such faith strives to rise above personal needs. Examples of this approach are reflected in: "My religious beliefs are what really lie behind my whole approach to life" (Allport, 1966, p. 6).

Empirically, however, a third group and pattern is indicated. Allport refers to them as "inconsistently proreligious." They generally like religion and they accept both intrinsically and extrinsically worded statements, although these may be contradictory. For this group, religion has social desirability.

Allport's (1950, 1960) distinction between the types of religiousness is not merely the extent of a person's religious behavior, but motives for his behavior, and to some extent, the consequences of his religious behavior in other aspects of his life.

Lenski (1963) also defined religious commitment in two ways. He distinguished between the socioreligious group, which involves the commitment of individuals to a group, and the commitment to a type of religious orientation which is highly individualistic and transcends group lines. The individualist orientation stresses the solitariness of the religious actor. The collectivist orientation stresses the importance of collective corporate religious activity. Basically, Allport and Lenski have similar dichotomies but assign different terms to these religious orientations.

Glock (1962) delineated five dimensions of commitment or "religiosity" as different ways in which an individual can be religious. These include: (1) religious belief as the ideological dimension, which includes the specific doctrines about what people believe and think about religion; (2) religious practice; as the ritualistic dimension, which includes participation and attendance at worship services, but takes into account the variations which exist in particular forms of religious practice; (3) religious feeling as the experiential dimension, which includes the subjective element of direct knowledge as a religious emotion of assurance; (4) religious knowledge as the intellectual dimension, which includes how much participants know about their religion; and finally, (5) religious effects as the consequential dimension, which includes the implications for practical conduct, reward, and responsibility. This is what the participant is expected to do and receive because of his religious commitment.

Glock concluded that researchers must focus on the interrelatedness of these dimensions. These areas are not independent but interdependent and must be measured together if the degree of commitment is to be determined. Glock did not suggest that highly committed participants would score high on a measure in every dimension. In fact, he cited Fukuyama's (1962) study showing that those who scored high on ritual observance and religious knowledge tended to score low on religious belief and feeling (Stark and Glock, 1968).

Fukuyama's (1962) study developed a typology according to types of religious participation. The four major styles he identified are: (1) the intellectually oriented, participants who are well informed and view the sermon as something to think about; (2) the organizationally oriented, participants who are active and faithful in attendance and contribution to the church; (3) the belief oriented, participants who consider beliefs important in defining their religious position; (4) the devotionally oriented, participants who emphasize feeling and emotion - the experiential part of religion.

The position of American psychology regarding religion has been a puzzling one. With the notable exceptions of William James (1902), Gordon Allport (1950), and a few others, most of psychology's key figures have ignored religious commitment and experience as worthy of investigation. Except for a small peripheral group of people who have done research on the psychology of religion, most American psychologists have preferred to disregard religion or to adopt an antagonistic position such as was heralded by Freud (1913).

In Search of a Soul

The integration of practice and knowledge with belief and experience is the road to spirituality. This unity is experienced as a fusion with God and an obliteration of the self.

Throughout the history of Judaism various movements have arisen, both from within and without Judaism, that have emphasized the road to spirituality by bifurcating body and soul, manifestation and essence, flesh and spirit, humanity and divinity, and extrinsic and intrinsic religious orientation.

From within Judaism, the Essenes strived for spirituality while emphasizing a life of asceticism. The Reform movement which arose in the 19th century accentuated the prophetic vision of social justice without the normative structure of Halakhah.

From without Judaism, Christianity arose from striving to achieve spirituality without the "form" of Halakhah as well.

Similarly within Orthodoxy, two groups started in the 18th century which indicated different emphases. The Hasidic movement stressed the simple man's way of reaching God through feeling even if it is devoid of knowledge as exemplified by the following anecdote:

59

Opening the Gates of Repentance

A young illiterate herdsman who lived alone during the year came on the Day of Atonement to the synagogue of the Baal Shem Tov. Although the lad was unable to join the congregation in prayer, he grasped the significance and spirit of the occasion as the day wore on. He experienced a strong, overwhelming emotion to participate with the congregation in pleading for atonement. As the Ne'ilah service was drawing to a close, the herdsman took from his pocket a reed whistle he used while tending his flock and blew on it lustily.

Hearing the solemn sanctity of the Ne'ilah thus disturbed, the Hasidim angrily upbraided the lad. However, the Baal Shem Tov, in a calm, decisive voice, took his followers to task:

Despite all your prayers, your learning and piety, you have not learned to repent, nor have you been able to prevail upon God to grant you pardon. This illiterate young herdsman, possessed with a sincere desire to serve the Almighty, has opened the gates of repentance for all of us.

The Hasidic movement also emphasizes the enjoyment of life in the performance of Halakhah. Nevertheless certain Hasidic sects are antinomian, particularly in reference to specific times of the morning, afternoon and evening prayers.

The movement that Hasidut arose against is known as the Mitnagdim, those who scrupulously observe every detail of Halakhah. Through this observance of all minutiae, these observant people feel that they are fulfilling the will of God. Anecdotes reflecting this movement have been mentioned previously in describing Rabbi Joseph Soloveitchik. The Mitnagdim ascribe 'objective' meaning to their observance but unfortunately do not necessarily imbue their behavior with ostensible subjective piety, spirituality, or emotions.

The Unity of Humanity and Divinity

The experience of striving for the numinous requires a special preparation of time and centering. It can take place both with a group, with a dyad or by oneself. But it always takes place with a source of fusion between man and God. This fusion is of a transient duration and usually eludes the modern Jewish person. Why? In order to achieve this union one has to be aware of one's psyche. The word 'psyche' is a Greek word connoting man's soul or spirit.

Modern man is frequently insufficiently aware of himself. Modern man is so easily distracted and frequently deceives

60

himself from the truth of himself alone or in a relationship. Modern man has much difficulty in centering and focusing.

The Torah indicates very few examples of the numinous experience. Not only are there few numinous experiences, their absence is particularly noteworthy. Not one numinous expression in the creation of the world! Not one numinous expression in the Akeda (Abraham's sacrifice of Isaac) story!!

A few numinous experiences which are mentioned in the Torah are noteworthy.

In Exodus 3:6, after an angel of God appears to Moses via a burning bush, Moses conceals his face because he is afraid to look at God. This experience is so overwhelming for Moses that his first reaction is to recoil from the reality of the experience. Moses reacts to God's presence by attemping to diminish this experience.

In Genesis 17:3, prior to Avram's metamorphosis to Abraham, Avram falls on his face when he hears that his children will continue the covenant that was between God and Abraham. Interestingly, despite Abraham's trepidation, God continues His discourse with him as if He was unaware of Abraham's religious experience.

In Deuteronomy 5:22-25, the people request never again to listen to God's voice because the experience of the theophany is too overwhelming and the people are afraid that they will die. Therefore, henceforth God will speak to the people via a prophet.

Perhaps Rudolph Otto's thesis in the Idea Of The Holy is demonstrated in the Bible. Otto maintains that the numinous is ineffable and any attempt at describing it not only falls short but actually does it injustice.

Why is Man Destined to Die?

The thesis of this paper is that the creation of man constitutes an attempt in unification of man and God, spirit and flesh. This creation of diametrically opposed entities can only coexist for a finite time period. Man is given the opportunity to strive for unity, to struggle against over-whelming difficult odds to achieve a balance whereby flesh is in service of spirit and spirit is in service of flesh.

Recognizing the insurmountable challenge which God has given man, God states in Genesis 6:3, "My Spirit shall not be in man forever since he is also composed of flesh, therefore his days shall be 120 years." God recognizes the ultimate

61

futility of eternal coexistence of diametrically opposite forces.

The Ultimate Challenge

Gabriel Marcel (1950), a French existentialist, stated that "Life is not a problem to be solved but a challenge to be lived." Rabbi Joseph Soloveitchik (1944) stated that "Against my will I was born and against my will I will die, but through my will I will live." These two terse but very poignant statements reflect my philosophy as well. Man, by recognizing the difficulty in his existence, has achieved a heightened awareness of God, man, and life. Through this new realization man continues the ultimate struggle of searching for permanent unity of body and soul in a transient time of 120 years.

References

Allport, G.W. (1950). The Individual and His Religion: A Psychological Interpretation. New York: MacMillan.

Allport, G.W. (1960). Religion in the Developing Personality. New York: University Press.

Allport, G.W. (1966). "Traits Revisited," American Psychologist. 21.

Freud, S. (1950). Totem and Taboo. London: Routledge and Kegan Paul. Originally published 1913.

Fukuyama, Y. (1961). "The Major Dimensions of Church Membership," Review of Religious Research. 2.

Glock, C.Y. (1962). "On the Study of Religious Commitment," Religious Education, Research Supplement. 57.

Heller, A.L. (Hebrew year: 5720). Kezot ha-Hoshen. Jerusalem: Pardes.

James, W. (1902). The Varieties of Religious Experience. New York: Dolphin Books.

Leeuw, G. van der. (1963). Religion in Essence and Manifestation. New York: Harper. Originally published 1933.

Lenski, G. (1963). The Religious Factor. New York: Doubleday and Co.

Marcel, G. (1950). The Mystery of Being. Chicago: Regnery.

Otto, R. (1967). The Idea of the Holy. New York: Oxford University Press. Originally published 1923.

Soloveitchik, J.B. (1983). Halakhic Man. Philadelphia: Jewish Publication Society.

Twersky, I. (1974). "Religion and Law," Religion in a Religious Age. S.D. Goitein (Ed.). Cambridge, Massachusetts: Ktav Publishing House.

CHAPTER 4

Integration of Roles of Rabbi and Psychotherapist

Introduction

My rabbinic functions have been modified as a result of my
training in psychotherapy (Ph.D. in psychology), and my
psychotherapeutic relationships have taken their own unique
form as a result of my being a rabbi. This process of
adaptation and accommodation of two distinct and unique
disciplines in striving to create an integrated whole has been
a creative inner struggle for me.

The Problem of Religion and Psychotherapy:
    As a rabbi, I feel three momentous forces pulling at me:
Halakhah, the Jewish covenantal community, and a continuous
oral and written tradition dating back from our teacher, Moses.
As a psychotherapist, I feel different forces have a direct
effect on my perceptions: the modeling effect of my professors
and clinical supervisors; a sense of being authentic to the
orientation of theistic existential psychotherapy - in which I
create my own essence and meaning for myself alone and in
relationship to others; and a sense of creativity and
individuality when relating to new patients.

Jewish Factors

Halakhah:
    The momentous forces guiding my Jewish clerical background
and my psychotherapeutic relationships require amplification.
Halakhah is the "Jewish Way" of life. Guidelines have been
established so that a person knows what to do in every
circumstance of life. Whether it be an issue of respect and
honor of one's parents or an issue of euthanasia, Halakhah has
specific guidelines. These guidelines have the sanction of God
Himself, although man has transmitted and codified the law
according to his own understanding (Deuteronomy 17:10; Heller,
5720).

The Covenantal Community:
    The Jewish covenantal community is the lay and rabbinic
body that I encounter. As an ordained rabbi, I and my
professional colleagues frequently serve, perhaps unknowingly
and even unwillingly as an evaluative body for our
constituency. Any deviation from the normative practice raises
questions and statements such as:

64

1. Did you consult our teacher, our master?
2. Who are you to take such an initiative upon yourself?
   (People with creativity are usually accused of causing
   a revolution (Kuhn, 1970)).
3. You apparently have deviated from our normative range
   of practices.
4. Your position represents a religiously leftist view.

From the lay community, sometimes articulated and sometimes
unarticulated points of view emerge. They take varied forms,
such as:

1. Our grandparents acted differently. Why can we not
   follow their precedent?
2. Rabbi, we live in America now! Why do you act as if
   you live in pre-World War II Europe?
3. Where is your sense of the aesthetic?

Some of these sentiments are mixed with expressions of awe and
respect felt by the speaker communicating with a rabbi.
Therefore, the statements may not be as direct as those
outlined above, but the underlying meanings are still there.

Tradition:
    The chain of tradition gives the clergy a tremendous sense
of security and stability. Here am I, knowing that there has
been an unbroken chain of tradition from my teacher to
Maimonides, to Hillel, to Ezra, to Joshua, and to Moses. What
a sense of privilege to be a part of that chain and at the same
time what an awesome sense of humility and responsibility to
sustain the age-old tradition without deviations or "new
traditions". Perhaps, however, our rabbis, themselves, created
temporary new tradition without setting a precedent when they
said, "This is the law, however, we do not publicize it to the
laity" (Talmudic Encyclopedia, 1959).

    Members of the clergy need to have professional and lay
companionship, sanction, and recognition. How burdensome it is
to be alone from your professional groups and friends. Can the
clergy's psychosocial needs be met by creating a new discipline
of clergy/psychotherapist? If not, is this creative process
worth the sacrifice?

Therapeutic Factors

Modeling:
    In addition to these traditional factors, current and
creative forces have influenced me as a psychotherapist.
Having trained under competent and sincere psychotherapists, I
have tried both consciously and unconsciously to incorporate
their varied counseling approaches. Those aspects which were

compatible with my way of life - such as empathy, care, and warmth (Truax and Carkhuff, 1967) - were readily adapted. Other aspects that were foreign to my rabbinic training - such as a specific 50 minute therapeutic hour, not initiating a call to a client to inquire about his/her welfare, touching a client whenever appropriate, and being non-directive - were attitudes that were uncomfortable for me.

Authenticity and Creativity:
   In addition to the social learning and modeling aspect that influenced me, the issue of a therapist's authenticity has had significant influence on me. Being authentic means responding with my total presence to the inquiry and inquirer. Responding in such fashion implies that:

   1. not everyone in similar situations responds in the same manner, and
   2. since I feel different on different days, my authenticity changes, as do my responses.

An authentic response may conflict with Jewish tradition. Despite the fact that the Jewish tradition has always emphasized integrity and truthfulness, an authentic response may differ from a traditional response.

   I feel elated when I am in the process of being creative with my clients in their various situations. This sense of creativity and unpredictability is tempered with my desire to maintain the Jewish tradition. Can one be traditional and creative in the same process?

Clinical Cases and Issues

   These different perspectives are operational in the following episodes that have taken place in the course of my pastoral counseling.

Conversion and Ritual Circumcision:
   According to traditional Jewish law, a person is Jewish if he either is born to a Jewish mother, or if he converts according to Jewish law. The basic requirements of conversion are:

   1. acceptance of the rule of the Kingdom of heaven,
   2. ritual circumcision (for males), and
   3. immersion in a ritual pool (Mikvah)
       (Karo, Shulhan Arukh, Yoreh Deah 268).

Case: A Jewish young man married a young woman who was converted by a rabbi, but one or both of the requirements for conversion were missing. As a result, the woman is still considered gentile. Their son is consequently considered a gentile, since he was born to a gentile mother. The mother, who presented herself as Jewish, requested a ritual circumcision for her son. The Mohel (traditional circumciser), who perceived the mother as a gentile, felt that the newborn son, a Gentile, did not require a ritual circumcision.

A Rabbinic authority was consulted and came to the following decision:

> In order not to contribute to the widening gap between the various (Reform, Conservative, and Orthodox) Jewish groups, a ritual circumcision should be performed and this should be the first step toward the child's and mother's real conversion. The overriding concern is peace within the entire Jewish community and carrying out properly the first step of the conversion process. The Mohel should instruct the parents to immerse the baby with the mother. Naturally the mother has to take upon herself the "rule of the Kingdom of heaven." (Tendler, 1978)

In many cases a mother has no intention to "really" convert or to immerse her child in a ritual pool. Frequently, what actually happens is that there is a decision such as that described above, without any follow-up to the final stages of conversion. The Rabbinic authority quoted above further stated that: "The responsibility of the Mohel is only at this point - but not to see the conversion through" (Tendler, 1978).

Should the Mohel not disqualify himself from the case if he knows that the parents are not going to conclude the conversion process? Is peace within the Jewish community based on a deceptive process? Are deceptive means allowed for "holy ends"? Where is the authenticity of the parents? Are they using the Mohel for their holy purposes?

This story relates to the question of whether "ends justify means". Judaism has always maintained that the process must be congruent with the achievement of the Torah goals. Knowing that conversion will not be completed but starting it nevertheless seems contrary to "pursuing holiness" (Leviticus 19:2), as well as to William James's (1902) concept of a religious conversion. Can peace be maintained with such a process?

Code or No Code:

A second issue which inherently poses conflict between religious and psychological influence is the case of resuscitating a terminally-ill cancer patient who has had a cardiac or respiratory arrest. This issue of No Code (DNR-Do Not Resuscitate) is a very complex issue both Halakhically and psychologically (Meier, 1982). The paradigm situation where

67

the problem occurs is when a patient who has terminal cancer has a cardiac or respiratory arrest. In such a situation, do the physicians have an obligation to attempt to revive the person? Religiously, the quality of life is not something that can be evaluated. Judaism maintains that wherever life exists, even when accompanied by pain and suffering, it is still life (Karo, Shulhan Arukh, Yoreh Deah 339:1). Many physicians feel differently. I feel very lonely with my values. Physicians maintain that the guilt of family members is their motivating factor in requesting the medical team to resuscitate the patient. They claim that a family's lifetime guilt is mitigated by insisting on heroic measures in helping to maintain the patient's life. They say that I do not attend to the real feelings of the family members. Perhaps I don't in some situations. In this matter of life and death, I act as a lonely man of faith (Soloveitchik, 1965) and abide with the religious tradition. Sometimes a family's real feelings are expressed after a person's death (Lo and Jonsen, 1980). Half a year after a terminal cancer patient had died, the family returned to the attending physician and asked, "Why did we so readily agree to no treatment as the patient had requested?"

A "Therapeutic Hour:"
Professionally, a therapist sees a client for 45, 50, 55, or 60 minutes. Usually, confining a session to the "hour" is considered a cardinal principle. Diminishing or increasing the therapeutic hour is distractive to the patient and is easily the cause of positive or negative transference. If the hour is extended, the transference may involve the patient's attraction to the therapist or the therapist's countertransference feelings for the patient.

If major psychological issues arise in the last moments of the therapeutic hour, the therapist should communicate the appropriate process to the client. However, if the entire session is involved and terminating the hour would be abrupt, the session should be extended when other patients are not waiting. Why? The Jewish people are the children of Abraham, representing mercifulness and kindness. That mercifulness and kindness supersede the professional therapeutic hour and reflect deep caring and concern for the client. How could a therapist act otherwise? Naturally the therapist must be aware that mercifulness and kindness are not motivated by a countertransferential reaction (Spero, 1980).

Caring for the client includes calling the client to inquire about his or her welfare. Following clients' cases in such a manner recognizes their needs.

Value-Oriented Therapy:
The question of directiveness and value-oriented therapy is at the crux of the religious-psychotherapeutic issue. A therapist tries to be aware of his own values, attitudes, and biases. By being aware of his own Weltanschauung, the therapist is careful not to impose his values on the client. Yet, certain values are conveyed just by the way the therapist acts. Behaviors such as the way one greets people, general attire, facial expressions, and the manner in which the therapist shows emotion, all convey values.

However, in other areas of human values and interaction, the therapist may keep his values to himself. Generally, psychotherapeutic theory maintains that in certain areas, such as beliefs about marriage, family, profession, and recreation, the therapist should not influence the client with a value that may not be compatible with the client's personality or psyche.

I feel that the imparting of these values is appropriate as possible alternatives at appropriate times within therapy. They can either be verbally articulated or expressed as the therapist's way of life. Obviously not every alternative that works for the therapist or one client will work for the next client. But the imparting of knowledge allows the client to evaluate alternative approaches.

Having presented pastoral and psychological situations in which different religious and therapeutic dimensions co-exist, I would like to now examine in detail one Torah commandment that illustrates my integration of religion and psychology as a model for a therapeutic relationship.

Rebuke and Reproof

The Commandment: Rebuke and Reproof:
"You shall not hate your brother in your heart, you shall surely rebuke your neighbor and do not commit a sin thereby" (Leviticus 19:17). This powerful and descriptive sentence expresses man's moral relationship with his fellow man. Maimonides (1178) explains this commandment to include:

1. confronting one's fellow with personal grievances held against him, and
2. reproaching evildoers in the hope of bringing about their improvement (Deot 6:6,7).

The intent of the rebuke is to establish a harmonious relationship between the person who erred and the person who was wronged. The duty to rebuke applies also to someone not hurt directly by evildoers, but who sees another straying from the path of the Torah. In order to achieve a harmonious relationship between the two individuals, a process is delineated which has many aspects common to a counseling relationship.

Referring to this process, the Talmud (Arakhin 16b) states that this attempt to rehabilitate should not embarrass an individual. It must be conducted in total privacy, by means of gentle words and an understanding disposition (Maimonides, 1178, Deot 6:7). This delicate process should only be undertaken with a person who appears amenable to change as a result of the process (Yebamot 65b and Proverbs 9:8).

All Israelites have responsibility for one another (Talmud, Shavuot 39a and Rosh Hashanah 29a). Everyone serves as a model for his fellow human being. Beyond this concept of modeling is the opportunity for rebuke and reproof. This communal responsibility has both altruistic and personal motivating factors. Altruistically, the motivating factor is helping another person in search of an alternative life style. On a personal level man's repentance process has an effect on himself, his community, and indeed, the entire world, according to Maimonides (1178, Teshubah 3:1-4).

Being amenable to change means being open to look at oneself. Someone who believes he has answers to all problems will not only refuse to increase his self-awareness, but will create distance between himself and the one who offers criticism (Proverbs 9:8). The result will be more enmity between these two people. Not only must the recipient of criticism be open to self-examination, but also he who rebukes must have certain characteristics. One should never point out a small flaw in another person when he himself has obvious shortcomings and deficiencies. This is important to such an extent that Rabbi Eleazar ben Azariah said, "I wonder if there is one in this generation who knows how to reprove," (i.e., who has such perfect qualities himself and is so sensitive to other people's feelings that he can criticize others (Talmud, Arakhin 16b).

However, if a person has such sensitivity and is able to say "let me point out this error in your otherwise good character," he will receive a blessing (Talmud, Tamid 28a and Proverbs 24:25).

The Implication for Counseling:
Distilling salient points from this Divine law and theology and applying it to a counseling relationship is instructive. The analogous aspects of the commandment of rebuke and the therapeutic relationship relate to the qualities of the therapist; the process of communication; the necessary

qualities of a receptive client; and the ability of the therapist to utilize transference and countertransference.

The necessary components of a successful therapist include the ability to assess one's life, in order to be aware of personal strengths, deficiencies, and vulnerabilities. A therapist should be able to utilize his shortcomings in order to be able to relate more effectively to himself and to his client. No one is expected to solve all of one's problems, but one is definitely required to be responsible for who he is and to be able to utilize that identity when relating to a client. Only under these circumstances can one truly listen and "be with" a client.

The process of communication is as significant as that which is said. This process requires: gentle words, an understanding and empathic disposition, and maintaining respect for the client while working together.

Gentle words indicate care, concern, warmth, and friendship. The client who feels these qualities will usually respond in kind and build a trusting relationship. The process must also build the client's self-esteem, by indicating many good attributes that the client has despite the particular issue at hand.

Not every client can be worked with. If a person is self-righteous and not interested in exploring his life, therapy is inappropriate for the time being. Clients must at least be open to dialogue.

Central to any therapeutic relationship is the client's transference and the therapist's countertransference. This process requires authenticity on the part of the therapist, as well as risk-taking. But is this not what we are asking of the client? We must require the same degree of openness in ourselves.

Integrated Views:
With this philosophy as a model, an integrated and wholesome view of religion and therapy can be established. Halakhah and tradition contain the key elements of a therapeutic relationship. Jewish law tells us to be non-judgmental, when doing so will create distance. Also, when the time is ready to accentuate a client's "new self-awareness," this can only be done by a very sensitive, self-aware therapist who can see through the eyes of the client. Therapeutic relationships are risky and creative because they are unpredictable. Whatever countertransference takes place will enable both the therapist and client to grow and develop. This process is indigenous to creativity and authenticity An

71

integrated view of religion and psychology requires an open look at the therapist's process. Contrary to a view of some religious psychotherapeutic integrationists, who view integration as the end product and result of the client's religious well-being, this paper has focused on the therapist's process of integration. The commandment of rebuke and reproof emphasizes the process, not the end result. Therapy should not be started with someone who appears not to be amenable to an open dialogue and a fresh approach to self-awareness. This view of integration emphasizes:

1. the therapist's self-analysis which assisted and guided him in an integrated view of religion and psychotherapy,
2. the therapist's ability to raise his consciousness and subsequently the client's religious and psychotherapeutic transferences and counter-transferences, and
3. the therapist's serving as an exemplary model of religious values in his own life and his ability to express these values.

Although each individual client represents different situations and unique conflicts between religion and mental health, the focus of integrated therapy is on the <u>therapist's</u> integration of religion and psychotherapy and on the therapeutic process between therapist and client.

Accentuating the aspect of individualizing the psychotherapeutic process is the commandment of "Before a blind man you should not place a stumbling block" (Leviticus 19:14). This passage is beautifully interpreted as not giving advice which is not suitable to someone at a particular time (Sifra 88). Not only is it inappropriate to give incorrect advice, but also one has to have an understanding of the client's <u>Weltanschauung</u> so that even "neutral advice and self-reflection" is suitable for the client's larger perspective. That which may be suitable when the therapeutic relationship is well-established may be premature at the early stage of the relationship. The client has to be seen as developing a greater self-awareness gradually. Torah values which have been modeled or expressed may be absorbed by the client at an appropriate time.

This process of integrating psychotherapy and religion has been creative for me and has enhanced each discipline in creating an holistic approach for someone who is both a rabbi and psychotherapist.

References

The Holy Scriptures (1985). Philadelphia: Jewish Publication Society.

James, W. (1902). The Varieties of Religious Experience. New York: Dolphin Books.

Karo, J. (16th Century). (1965). Shulhan Arukh. New York: M.P. Press.

Kuhn, T. (1970). The Structure of Scientific Revolutions. Chicago: University of Chicago Press.

Lo, B., and Jonsen, A.R. (1980). "Ethical Decisions in the Care of a Patient Terminally Ill with Metastatic Cancer," Annals of Internal Med. 92.

Maimonides, M. (12th Century) (1962). Book of Knowledge. Translated by M. Hyamson, Jerusalem: Boys Town.

Meier, L. (1982). "Code and No-Code: A Psychological Analysis and the Viewpoint of Jewish Law, "Legal and Ethical Aspects of Treatment for the Critically and Terminally Ill Patient. Michigan: American Society of Law and Medicine, and Health Administration Press of the University of Michigan.

Sifra. (1946). New York: Om Publishing Company.

Soloveitchik, J.B. (1965). "The Lonely Man of Faith," Tradition, 7, (2).

Spero, M. (1980). Judaism and Psychology: Halakhic Perspectives. New York: Ktav Publishing House, Inc. and Yeshiva University Press.

Talmudic Encyclopedia. (1959). Volume 9, Jerusalem: Talmudic Encyclopedia Publishing Ltd.

Tendler, M. (1978). Written and oral communication.

The Talmud (18 Volumes). (1961). Edited by I. Epstein. London: Soncino Press.

The Talmud (Jerusalem). (Hebrew year: 5582). Venice.

Traux, C.B., and Carkhuff, R.R. (1967). Toward Effective Counseling and Psychotherapy: Training and Practice. Chicago: Aldine.

CHAPTER 5

The Loneliness-Togetherness Dialectic:

A Psycho-Judaic Perspective

Introduction

I am writing this essay at a time in my life that Carl
Gustav Jung referred to as the time of a person's greatest
potential psychological and spiritual growth (Jung,1933, pp.
95-114). At this juncture of life, commonly referred to as the
period of a mid-life crisis, many assumptions are reevaluated
and insights are analyzed from new and different perspectives.
My life has been blessed and I feel a great sense of gratitude
and appreciation to God. My wife and I have four healthy and
beautiful children and the continuous challenges which they
present further stimulate our own development. Educationally,
I have received Rabbinic ordination from Yeshiva University and
subsequently, a doctorate in psychology from the University of
Southern California. These two distinct fields complement each
other as I render pastoral/psychological counseling to hospital
patients and private clients. I have had the distinct privilege of serving as the Jewish Chaplain at Cedars-Sinai Medical
Center in Los Angeles for the past ten years. In that capacity, I have assisted innumerable patients and their families in
almost every conceivable medical and psychological situation.
Among those I have encountered, the most significant and
critical events revolve around the caring for terminally ill
patients and their families. Through these experiences, my
awareness and sensitivity to the fragility of life and the
inevitability of death have become extremely heightened. The
personal impact of all this has left an indelible impression.
As a psychologist, I have been aware that just as the unique
therapeutic relationship has served as a major part of the
healing process for clients, it has also provided me, as the
healer, with new insights into my own psychodynamic behavior.
In both capacities, I have been personally enriched by the
human services that I have been privileged to provide. The
trust, confidence and enduring friendships that have resulted
have become part of a permanent treasure that I will always
fondly cherish and remember, and that will serve as an eternal
inspiration to me.

At the same time I also feel lonely. This loneliness
should be clinically differentiated from aloneness, alienation
or depression. Aloneness, alienation and depression may contain aspects of loneliness; however, loneliness may exist as a
distinct state independent from any other emotional feeling or
mental condition. In a widely acclaimed and often-quoted classic article entitled "The Lonely Man of Faith" Rabbi Joseph B.

74

Soloveitchik (1965) writes from a theological-Biblical perspective, but not from a psychological-empirical point of view (p. 9). The word loneliness, however, conveys a psychological construct as it relates to the human condition. Loneliness is an emotion which manifests itself in many different situations. One can be lonely among friends and one can be spiritually lonely. It can occur only when one thinks about oneself. The content of loneliness is unique in that thought and feeling are of such a private nature that the person feels inhibited to share that intimacy with anyone. Loneliness is the combination of a thought, a feeling of intense uniqueness, and a metacognition on the thought and feeling. The metathought is a reflection on a reflection. This introspection represents an evaluation of one's thought and feeling processes. The self becomes an object of analysis.

The experience of spiritual loneliness is of a different nature. The inability to experience the presence of God is a reaction to one's constant search consciously or subconsciously for a renewed meaning in life. This feeling can occur during happy moments or unanticipated tragedies, frequently or of long duration, intermittently or continuously. This feeling is usually precipitated by a gradual and/or sudden incomprehensibility of one's place, role or fate in the world. A previous theory and value system has now been shown to be inadequate to explain or to understand one's experience of the here-and-now.

The commonality between human (i.e., psychological) and spiritual loneliness is the emotional feeling of differentness, uniqueness and singularity, while the differential factor is the subject of the human union. Human loneliness represents one's estrangement from one's fellow human beings, and spiritual loneliness is to exist in exile from the Divine.

The word and concept of loneliness can only exist with its antithesis - togetherness. Dark and light, and evil and good are classic antinomies that shed meaning on one another. Lonely and together also represent an antinomy. Human togetherness is the ability to share one's being with another. It is a feeling of unity and union. Togetherness allows one to feel completely understood by another. The singularity, uniqueness and loneliness, is transformed into a dyadic oneness. This dyad, or enlarged oneness, represents a microcosm of universal and cosmic oneness. Each person is indeed comparable to a whole world.

The Mishnah states (Sanhedrin 4:5), that saving a single life is conceptually comparable to creating a whole world. Every individual represents a small world (Olam Katan), a microcosm. Knowing oneself becomes identical with knowing a total being. Isaac Israeli, a neoplatonic medieval Jewish

75

philosopher, stated: "This being so, it is clear that man, if he knows himself in both his spirituality and corporeality, comprises knowledge of all, and knows both the spiritual and corporeal substance, and also knows the first substance which is created from the power of the Creator without mediator..." (Altmann and Stern, 1958, p.27). When a person shares a special part of the psyche with another, it feels comparable to a unique cosmic unity of togetherness. This feeling is soothing. The moments of togetherness may only be of a short duration, even a fleeting moment, but their impact is ever-lasting. Even in moments of intense loneliness, the experience of togetherness is remembered. This loneliness-togetherness dialectic represents the three ways that life is experienced: lonely, together, and lonely-together and together -lonely.

In sharp contrast to the loneliness-togetherness dialectic, there stands the state of aloneness. Being alone refers to the absence of contact with another person. Being alone is frequently associated with widows, widowers or other people who live by themselves. People who live alone are not necessarily lonely. If so, it is independent of their aloneness. Loneliness refers to their psyche's state, while aloneness refers to a lack of companionship.

The loneliness-togetherness dialectic finds expression in many diverse aspects of life. Relationships, with particular emphasis on family relationships, are the primary manifestation of the loneliness-togetherness dialectic. Another area of the dialectic includes one's relationship with God. Naturally, the relationships with God, friends, and family change over the course of one's life. At moments of bliss or of tragedy, the loneliness-togetherness dialectic takes on a unique nature.

This nature is constantly evolving, depending on the circumstances and a person's frame of mind at a particular time and place. However, the common denominator is the loneliness-togetherness dialectic. This dialectic ultimately can serve as a springboard for a greater understanding and refinement of the self, enabling one to further develop both spiritually and psychologically. The loneliness-togetherness dialectic can also be a point of departure for creativity. Many creative works are conceived in states of loneliness. This loneliness may also continue after the creative processes, since the creator's contemporaries often have a hard time accepting what the lonely creator has had to share (Fromm-Reichman, 1959, p. 326).

The quintessential state of loneliness encompasses both reflections on the past and anticipatory feelings about the future. Present loneliness focuses exclusively on desolate phases of past relationships. The significant and meaningful relationships of the past are either forgotten or reconstructed

76

and perceived inappropriately. Future positive relationships are out of the realm of expectation or imagination. This past and future which merge with the present comprise the incommunicable aspect of the present loneliness. This approach corresponds to Beck's depression inventory items - sense of failure and pessimism. The retrospective sense of failure is represented by "as I look back on my life, all I can see is a lot of failures." The futuristic pessimism is reflected by "I feel I have nothing to look forward to" (Beck and Beamesdorfer, 1974, pp. 167-169).

Loneliness and Tolerance

Although the loneliness-togetherness dialectic applies to all human beings of all races, nationalities, religions and cultures, the Jewish heritage accentuates a specific psychological, sociological, philosophical, and theological loneliness-togetherness dialectic.

I feel particularly lonely as a Jew. The Jewish people were chosen as a designated minority (Deuteronomy 7:7,8), as a small fragment of the whole of humanity. The Jewish people have always been few in numbers (currently, approximately 15 million Jews in a world population of several billion people), despite the Divine covenant (Genesis 13:16; 22:17) promising that the descendants of Abraham would multiply as the heavenly stars, the dust of the earth and the sand of the seashore. This minority people has been assigned the "burdensome privilege" of becoming a "kingdom of priests and a holy nation" (Exodus 19:6). The Jewish people's purpose is to be "a light to the nations" (Isaiah 42:6). They should serve as a moral and spiritual guide for all of humanity.

The Jewish people observe specific precepts which have been commanded by an incorporeal Divine being; however, the gentile people have been allotted the sun, moon, stars and other heavenly hosts to worship (Deuteronomy 4:19; 29:25). What is considered one of the three cardinal sins in Judaism, namely idolatry, is deemed as appropriate Divine worship for the gentile nations according to their state of historical development. Not only does the Jewish religion strongly negate the active proselytizing of gentiles, it strongly advocates the attitude of religious tolerance of other religions. Maimonides codifies this noble concept (Mishneh Torah, Melakhim 8:11):

A heathen who accepts the seven commandments and observes them scrupulously is a "righteous heathen," and will have a portion in the world to come, provided that he accepts them and performs them because the Holy One, blessed be He, commanded them in the Law and made known through Moses our Teacher that the observance thereof had been enjoined upon

77

the descendants of Noah even before the Law was given. But if his observance thereof is based upon a reasoned conclusion he is not deemed a resident alien, or one of the pious of the Gentiles, but one of their wise men. (Twersky, 1972, p. 221; Twersky, 1980, p. 455; Altmann, 1973, p. 294)

Maimonides equates the reward of a righteous gentile with that of a righteous Jew. The prophet Malachi (1:11) declares that sacrificial offerings of heathens are a glorification of God. The gentile nations that worship the sun, moon, and heavenly hosts ultimately pay tribute to a Divine being. The medieval Jewish poet and philosopher, Solomon ibn Gabirol, recognized that all sincere gentile worship is in reality offered to the one God of all the earth. He expressed this inspired thought:

Thou art the Lord, and all beings are Thy creatures, Thy domain;
And through those who serve idols vain,
Thine honor is not detracted from,
For they all aim to Thee to come. (quoted in Hertz, 1981, p.76)

The loneliness of the covenantal Jew is reflected in the fact that while fulfilling the chosen God-Abrahamic covenant of being a light to the nations (Exodus 19:6), one is aware that gentile observances are at times antithetical to Jewish values and laws, yet equally valid and sanctioned by God in the Bible. A Jew prays to an incorporeal God, while a gentile may worship the sun and the moon. A Jew observes the Sabbath on a Saturday with all of its meticulous details, while a gentile may observe Friday or Sunday as a holy day. A Jew eats only certain foods which the dietary laws allow, while a gentile may eat ham and bacon. Both the Jew and the gentile in their respective observances are considered pious individuals.

It is axiomatic that different religions have different behaviors and symbols in their religious life. This multiplicity of varied thoughts, actions and symbols allows for diverse avenues to serve God. This understanding leads to a refreshing religious tolerance and a complete rejection of religious exclusivity. Maimonides understands the rise of Christianity and Islam not in terms of a negation of Judaism nor in terms of daughter-religions of Judaism, but rather as assisting humanity in all parts of the world to believe in monotheism, regardless of their modes of worship, including doctrines and actions that are antithetical to Judaic tenets and dogmas. Maimonides states about Messianic aspiration (Mishneh Torah, Melakhim 11:4, the uncensored edition):

But it is beyond the human mind to fathom the designs

78

of the Creator; for our ways are not His ways, neither are our thoughts His thoughts. All these matters relating to Jesus of Nazareth and the Ishmaelite (Muhammad) who came after him only served to clear the way for King Messiah, to prepare the whole world to worship God with one accord, as it is written, "For then will I turn to the peoples a pure language, that they may all call upon the name of the Lord, to serve Him with one consent" (Zephaniah 3:9). Thus the Messianic hope, the Torah, and the commandments have become familiar topics - topics of conversation (among the inhabitants) of the far isles and many peoples, uncircumcised of heart and flesh. They are discussing these matters and the commandments of the Torah. Some say, "Those commandments were true, but have lost their validity and are no longer binding." Others declare that they had an esoteric meaning and were not intended to be taken literally; that the Messiah has already come and revealed their occult significance. But when the true King Messiah will appear and succeed, be exalted and lifted up, they will forthwith recant and realize that they have inherited naught but lies from their fathers, that their prophets and forebears led them astray. (Twersky, 1980, p.452)

Maimonides accords both Christianity and Islam a positive historical function to prepare the world for true monotheism and to serve God in a unified/together manner. However, until this Messianic era arrives, the Jew is perceived from within and without as a lonely worshipper of God among the vast majority of the people of the world who also worship God in their unique ways.

This perception of the Jewish people has served as a reason and an inexcusable justification for antisemitism. Haman justified his actions by declaring that the Jewish people's laws are different from those of every other people. (Esther 3:8).

This differentness and uniqueness of the Jewish people is rooted in the name of the first Jew, or to be more precise, the first Hebrew. The founder of the Jewish religion and the first patriarch is referred to as Abraham the Hebrew (HaIvri, Genesis 14:13.) One possible interpretation of the word Ivri is that it means 'one from the other side,' in accordance with the statement, "And I took your father Abraham from the other side of the river (Euphrates)" (Joshua 24:3). The Midrash (Midrash Rabbah, Genesis 42:8) implies that a Jew is always from 'the other side.' The Jew is always different. The Jew's attire and weltanschauung are singular. This is the fate and destiny of the Jew: to be different, to be a light to the nations, and to be a model of religious tolerance. The Jew feels that the whole world is on the other side of the river -- always the feeling of uniqueness coupled with the enlightened concept of religious tolerance of other modes of worship.

Abraham the Hebrew, Abraham HaIvri, Abraham, the 'one from the other side,' chose to listen to the Divine command of Lekh Lekha, to leave his country, his birthplace, and his father's home. Abraham had to sever all his connections so that he could fulfill his lifelong mission of being a blessing to all of mankind. (Genesis 12:1-4). In order for this noble goal to be accomplished, any contaminating influences (such as sacrificing children to the idol Molech) needed to be eliminated. To be isolated and lonely are the necessary preconditions to being a blessing to all of humanity. Abraham, and the Abraham in each one of us, must take leave of our country, our birthplace, and our father's home to become a blessing unto ourselves and a blessing for all others. Our country, birthplace, and father's home have their own "Terach's idols." Our idols do not necessarily have to be similar to the evil or heinous activities that surrounded Abraham. Our idols are those things which inhibit an autonomous sense of self. Our idols can be narcissism, greed, lust or the feelings of lack of self-worth or self-esteem that are so prevalent in our generation.

This process of separation or individuation is the most painful and yet the most significant development in entering mature adulthood. Individuation does not represent a rejection of parental and generational values, but rather a rebirth of self through self-examination. This rebirth is our own Lekh Lekha, our own path and road traveled.

This process entails a necessary loss of precious togetherness. However, this painful isolation and loneliness constitutes the first step in climbing one's own Jacob's ladder of ascension. Each ascending step, each forward move, is a move away from our country, birthplace and home. This necessary loneliness towards individuation brings blessings to all of humanity. Ultimately, the blessing is a togetherness of all nations, where all the families of the earth are blessed in unison and in unity.

There is also an added dimension in a Jew's process of individuation. The Jew accepts the privilege and yoke of being a light to the families of the earth. This differentness must not represent a holier-than-thou attitude, but on the contrary, the Jew must epitomize religious tolerance to all the different modes of worship. The Jew's loneliness is manifest in all facets of life. Yet, it is this distinctiveness that entices the nations of the world to take notice of the Jewish people. This distinctiveness overflows into areas of morality, righteousness and interpersonal relationships. Then, the individual Jew and the Jewish people collectively serve as an eternal beacon of light to all of humanity.

The Jew and the gentile have different modes of worship. However, as Barbra Streisand's (1974) lyrics state in "Being at War With Each Other:"

Everyone comes from

one Father, one Mother

so, why do we complicate our lives so much by being at war with each other....

All I know is everyone else is a sister or brother so we have to stop being at war with each other.

The Seven Noahide Laws

If we all come from one father, one mother, and we all are brothers and sisters to one another, why are Jewish law and gentile law seemingly diametrically opposed to one another? What does Judaism say about the scope of moral and legal responsibilities of the gentile nations? After the devastating punishment of the Flood, God established the first covenant with humanity. The covenant, a rainbow, affirmed that God will never again destroy all life by a flood. Furthermore, God established the seven laws of Noah. Rabbinic interpretation of Genesis 9:1-7 enumerates the fundamental laws of humanity as: the establishment of courts of justice, the prohibition of blasphemy, of idolatry, of incest, of bloodshed, of robbery, and of eating flesh cut from a living animal (Talmud, Sanhedrin 56a). These constitute what may be called natural religion -- that which is vital to the existence of human society. Prima facie, these seven Noahide laws appear in stark contrast to the 613 commandments of the Torah (Talmud,Makkot 23b). However, if one excludes all the laws that are operational and dependent upon the Temple in Jerusalem, the 613 commandments are reduced to 271 commandments (Kagan, 1958).

The seven Noahide laws represent significant legislative areas and each area encompasses numerous legal dicta. There are at least 66 Biblical laws that are within the rubric of the seven Noahide laws (Kagan, 1958).

The Noahide laws refer to seven broad areas of legislation. These represent an all-embracing system. This concept of an all-encompassing system to be structured around seven laws finds its parallel in the search to find all 613 Biblical laws rooted in the Ten Commandments, as Saadiah Gaon tried to do (Rosenberg, 1856, part II, p.39).

81

The seven Noahide categorical laws, the Ten Commandments, and the 271 laws of the Bible not related to the Temple and its services are the basic and yet all-encompassing ways that allow societies to exist and coexist with one another. From this perspective, the Jew is not lonely. On the contrary, the Jew has a leadership role in establishing ethical monotheism, which is not particularistic in nature but rather universal in aspiration.

Every nation has its unique historical origin. Jew and gentile alike strive to create a law-abiding society where all people struggle to live ethically based on their own specific Divine legal/moral systems.

The loneliness of the Jew reemerges in the observances of the unique laws of Judaism, known as Hukkim (statutes). Maimonides explains that it is specifically through the observance of Hukkim that eventually the gentile nations will recognize the wisdom and understanding of the Jewish people (Deuteronomy 4:6). Maimonides states in the Guide:

> Thus it states explicitly that even all the statutes (Hukk-im) will show to all the nations that they have been given with wisdom and understanding...every commandment from among these six hundred and thirteen commandments exists either with a view to communicating a correct opinion, or to putting an end to an unhealthy opinion, or to communicating a rule of justice, or to ward off an injustice, or to endowing men with a noble moral quality, or to warning them against an evil moral quality. (Maimonides, p.524)

The Hukkim accomplish one primary goal. The Jewish people are completely separated from the gentile nations. The Jewish people eat certain foods (dietary laws), dress uniquely (Shaatnez laws), and married couples are allowed to have sexual relations only during specific times of the woman's menstrual cycle (laws of family purity). These laws and all of the Hukkim are constant reminders of the differentness and singularity of the Jewish people. The experience of Jewish history seems to belittle the Jewish people's practice of the Hukkim. Instead of receiving admiration and respect from the other nations (Deuteronomy 4:6), the Jewish people have been typified as a "despised people" (HaLevi). Why does a people whose mission is to be a light to the nations require such separateness? This separateness has frequently served as an excuse for the hatred and persecution of Jews. In this separateness, I feel particularly lonely.

Jewish lore has likewise grappled with this issue. The Midrash states (Sifra, Leviticus 20:26) regarding the Hok of the dietary laws that a Jew should not say that the combination

82

of meat and milk or pork does not taste good, but rather that abstention from these foods is based on the prohibitions of the Bible and Talmud. The Midrash implies that it is reasonable and understandable to desire to eat milk and meat together, or to eat pork, or to do or abstain from any other Hok. The observance of Hukkim demonstrates uncompromising obedience to a Divine imperative. This Midrash emphasizes the significance of blind commitment to law rather than the intrinsic benefit and wisdom of law that gentile nations will ascribe to the observant Jewish people as Deuteronomy 4:6 indicates.

Why this separateness? Why this singularity? Why is the fate and destiny of the Jewish people unique and lonely? Why does the privilege of being a light to the nations contain within itself the burdensome loneliness of being a despised Jew?

Bilaam, a non-Jewish prophet, declares that Israel "is a people that shall dwell alone and shall not be reckoned among the nations" (Numbers 23:9). The Jewish people are isolated and distinguished from other peoples by their religious and moral laws and by the fact that they have been chosen as an instrument of Divine purpose.

This distinctiveness has been a point of contention for Jew and gentile alike. Some Jews resent their distinctiveness; some use it inappropriately, claiming that the Jews are a superior race. Some gentiles hate the Jews because of their chosenness and distinctiveness; most do not understand this concept.

A Theoretical Reconstruction of World Religious History

This burdensome and lonely distinctiveness can be understood if we momentarily entertain an antithetical construct of world religious history. Assume that no nation was granted the special status of "a light to the nations." Furthermore, assume that the Torah was revealed in a spectacular miraculous theophany to all nations together in a universal revelation. This new Torah or revelation would, of necessity, have a different content and description of the would-be new history. The main thrust of desired human ethical and moral behavior and religious symbols would be the same. However, any aspects of religious exclusivity or legal particularism would be eliminated.

Hukkim would not exist. The Torah would be the Divine revelation of a universal natural religion. This Divine natural religion would serve as a guide for personal fulfillment and interpersonal relations among individuals, families, societies and nations. A Divine natural religion differs from

83

a natural religion. A Divine natural religion emanates from a Divine being; a natural religion emanates from a universal human conscience. This theoretical Divine natural religion would apply to all different nationalities without any distinction.

This theoretical rewriting of the Divine natural religion is a facsimile of the actual natural religion which originated with the sons of Noah (Genesis 9:1-7). All the nations of the earth had their origin with the sons of Noah: Shem, Ham and Yafet. All the races known to the Israelites were arranged as if they were different branches of one great family. All the nations were represented as having originated from the same ancestry. All people were therefore brothers and sisters. This concept of the unity of the human race is an outgrowth of the belief in the unity of God. This is the true genesis of the Messianic idea. This Divine ideal of one humanity, united by a common natural religion, language, culture and ancestry living in tranquil coexistence was not realized (Genesis 11:1-9). Instead of enjoying the Divine presence among all people, humanity revolted against God. Temple-towers were built to immense height as if to challenge God's powers and exclusivity. A shrine of a deity was mounted on top of these temple-towers, symbolizing a war against the Deity.

The nature of humanity, both before and after the Flood, demonstrated that unbridled human nature has tremendous potential for destructiveness and evil. Before the Flood, God repented that humanity was created with such a propensity to evil and decided to destroy everything with the exception of Noah-the-righteous and his family. After the Flood and the further evil perpetrated by the extended family of Noah, God abandoned the idea of universal unity of the human race and began again, but this time not through a universal family, but rather through a particular family (Abraham) as a model for all of humanity.

Thus, by tentatively rewriting world religious history, it becomes clear that a universal religion and unity of all of humanity was indeed the original idea of God. After the attempted implementation of this Messianic idea which was constantly thwarted by the inner and basic core of human nature, God chose a different route, the route of having a chosen nation.

The Concept of A Chosen Nation

The concept of a chosen nation to be a light to the nations is based on the empirical failure of the initial unity of humanity. God has asked the Jewish people to be a singular and different people from all the people on the face of the earth. This lonely road will hopefully assist the Jewish people in the

84

development of a national and individual moral character. Negative external influences should be avoided at all costs. In order to accomplish this goal, the Jewish people observe Hukkim, whose primary goal is to keep the Jewish people as a separate people. This separateness has one exclusive goal: to assist God in achieving the original Divine plan, the unity of humanity under the parenthood of God and brotherhood of humanity. The initial plan of God to achieve the unity of humanity was thwarted twice -- once before the Flood and once after the Flood. Henceforth, this noble goal will be accomplished, but now through different means. When this ultimate goal is achieved, the nations will understand that this goal could only have been accomplished through a distinct and separate nation and that this distinctiveness and separateness could only have been accomplished through the observance of Hukkim (Deuteronomy 4:6). This interpretation differs from Maimonides' in an important way (Guide 3:31). For Maimonides, the Hukkim have intrinsic merit, wisdom and utility. For this author, the Hukkim's primary raison d'etre is to create a separate and unique nation that will be a light to all the other nations, specifically in the areas of universal ethics and morality.

The Hukkim, in and of themselves, may not have any intrinsic merit. Furthermore, it is inconceivable that a Divine Being would favor one people over another; indeed the Midrash regarding the dietary laws (Sifra, Leviticus 20:26) supports this thesis regarding the theoretical underpinnings of Hukkim. This does not exclude the possibility that Hukkim can have intrinsic wisdom and utility.

Utilizing this thesis, one can better comprehend Maimonides' statement regarding the role of Christianity and Islam in the constantly unfolding plan of history. Christianity and Islam are supposed to assist Judaism in instilling faith in one God and to help prepare the road for the coming of the Messiah (Mishneh Torah, Melakhim 11:4, the uncensored edition.)

Rabbi Yehudah HaLevi (1960,p.121) similarly expresses the purpose and function of Christianity and Islam. He states:

So it is concerning the religion of Moses: all later religions are transformed into it, though externally they may reject it. They merely serve to introduce and pave the way for the expected Messiah: he is the fruit; all will be his fruit, if they acknowledge him, and will become one tree. They then will revere the root they formerly despised... (1960,p.121)

Thus, separateness, distinctiveness and uniqueness are necessary components for a nation before it can accomplish its ultimate goal of being a light to the nations. This prelimi-

85

nary stage is necessary both on a collective national basis and on an individual basis. The burdensome and challenging loneliness of the observant Jew is a necessary precondition in humanity's historical evolution; the anticipated Messianic togetherness forms the special loneliness-togetherness dialectic.

Loneliness and Marital Intimacy

Eric Erikson has described the eight stages of a person's life. Significant in his description is the fact that each stage is also a necessary prerequisite to its successor. In order for there to be intimacy, a person's identity must be firmly established. Physiological growth, mental maturation and social responsibility are some of the phases that an adolescent passes through while struggling with the crisis of identity (Erikson, 1968 p.151).

What is meant by a person's identity and how is it achieved? Despite the constantly changing nature of identity, a basic core personality emerges during adolescence and young adulthood which continues throughout one's lifetime. The struggle of creating this identity requires an inner synthesis of what one has been and what one expects to be: of gender and sexual identity; ethical, ethnic, occupational, private and societal parts of oneself; of one's choices and dreams. Although identity formation and transformation continually grows and develops, it primarily rests on adolescents' and young adults' initial responses to their core personalities.

Adolescent and young adult individuation is based on parental modeling (which may or may not be acknowledged) and peer identification, in combination with the emergence of a new self. Boundaries are formed of who one is and who one is not. While the modeling and identification phases are in process, their opposing tendencies also contribute to the emergence of a new self. Rejection of certain parental values is equally significant in the formation of a new person. This "new individual" is usually accompanied by feelings of loneliness and isolation from his or her parents. Identification with one's peers is usually associated only with this phase of development, but not necessarily with the unique values, likes, tastes and limitations of others.

This phase of development, of the initial establishment of one's identity, is included in the Biblical pronouncement "therefore everyone should leave one's parents" (Genesis 2:24). The Targum supports this theory by underscoring that leaving one's parents requires moving out of one's parents' home. The Targum understood that a young adult's individual psyche requires one's own home.

86

Individuation and the formation of identity are necessary
for the next phase of development, called intimacy. The Bible
states "and one should cleave to one's wife and they shall be
one flesh" (Genesis 2:24). Fromm succinctly and poignantly
states that which is implicit in the Biblical expression of
"one flesh." He says that the art of loving is when "two
beings become one and yet remain two" (1956,p.17).

Even in blissful union, creative intimacy, altruistic
loving, orgastic release, and ultimate togetherness, one is
still aware of oneself as a separate entity and aloneness. The
achievement of self and individuation, which is a necessary
prerequisite for intimacy, brings at the same time the concomi-
tant and painful awareness of one's singular existence.

Fromm states:
Man is gifted with reason; he is _life being aware of it-
self_...

This awareness of himself as a separate entity, the awareness of his own short life span, of the fact that without
his will he is born and against his will he dies, that he
will die before those whom he loves, or they before him,
the awareness of his aloneness and separateness, of his
helplessness before the forces of nature and society, all
this makes his separate, disunited existence an unbearable
prison. He would become insane could he not liberate himself from this prison and reach out, unite...(1956,p.8)

The marital union is based on each person's struggle in the
process of becoming individuated and being together at the same
time. Each person's individuation may proceed according to
one's own time schedule and maturation. It is precisely this
awareness of distinctiveness and separateness that allows for
love, togetherness, union and intimacy. This loneliness-
togetherness dialectic reflects the most intimate moments of
marital and sexual relations.

The loneliness-togetherness of marital relations represents
a step towards completeness. The Bible states: "It is not
good for a person to be alone, I will make for one an _Ezer
K'negdo_" (Genesis 2:18). The word _Ezer_ literally means "help"
and the word _K'negdo_ literally means "in opposition (or
against) one's helpmate."

The Talmud has grappled with this dichotomous expression
(Yebamot 63a). The Talmud explains that if a person is meritorious, one's helpmate is helpful; if the contrary is true, then
one's spouse is a constant irritation. An alternate interpretation can suggest that mates can recognize their own uniqueness, singularity and differentness, while at the same time,

87

they can try to be helpful in promoting their partner's development. In that mutuality, togetherness will flourish.

In reality, all the interpretations (including the literal translations of the words) find expression in the marital relationship. At times, the bond between a husband and wife is reflective of complete harmony. At other times, the spousal relationship can reflect profound destructive tendencies, overtly or covertly.

Marital difficulties are not the result of "sick" people or immaturity, but rather reflect a human/marital pendulum of helpfulness and its antithesis. This reality mirrors the loneliness-togetherness dialectic. The Biblical expression for intimacy and sexual relations, Yada (knowledge) (Genesis 4:1), similarly represents the ambivalence of relationships. Knowledge of one's spouse can never be all-encompassing; it always contains elements of doubt and uncertainty. Faith and doubt, knowledge and uncertainty, and love and hostility are all part of the loneliness-togetherness marital relationship.

A deeper understanding of the enjoinder to know one's spouse is found when we take as a process of striving to constantly know one's mate in a more profound way. This process of striving brings blissful togetherness, along with the recognition that complete knowledge of the other can never be attained. Husband and wife, in their loneliness-togetherness dialectic, move from intimate lovers to intimate strangers. Just as no two other adults can become such intimate friends and lovers, it is equally true that no two other adults can be so potentially destructive to each other.

The Ultimate Lonely Search for Meaning

Ambiguities, ambivalences, doubts and uncertainties are an integral part of attempting to comprehend the loneliness-toge- therness dialectic of the Jew and gentile, as well as of the male-female marital relationship. After everything is said, the author and the readers still grapple with incomplete solu- tions and more esoteric challenges.

I would like to suggest (and this is not meant as an apolo- getic approach to life's complexities) that the insolubility of either a universal or particular meaning of life is the great- est benefit to all of humanity. Constant fluidity, meeting the perennial challenges of life and the eternal search for meaning, endows everyone with a potential raison d'etre - a meaningful existence. A parallel mode of making the best of insolvable challenges, is described in the formulation that death confirms meaning on life (see Chapter 8).

Life is not meant to be fully understood. The Bible states that no one, not even Moses, can see God and live (Exodus 33:20). God is unknowable. Ipso facto, human life, that which contains the image of God (Genesis 1:27), must also be unknow- able. If the ability to know oneself is unobtainable, allow me to suggest a new interpretation for the ancient maxim "know thyself." For everyone to continually search for life's meaning is the ultimate meaning of life. Even in old age, the criterion for good mental and physical health is "use it or lose it." Whatever the "it" refers to, (be it the search for knowledge, greater understanding of beauty or the ability to love), the emphasis is on the dynamic utilization of one's natural abilities.

When life becomes motionless, death has arrived. Even before one's final death, one encounters other types of "death." A stroke which causes the paralysis of the left side of the body results in a motionless arm and leg. Through phys- ical rehabilitation, life may be restored and movement may ensue. From the second that conception takes place, growth and development occur. Mobility, not stillness, represents the vitality of life.

Movement and vitality reflect the individual and subjective human endeavor in searching for meaning in life. All the people of the world, all religions, search for purpose and meaning. In this search, each individual is lonely, yet together with every other living person.

89

A Commitment to Togetherness

The therapeutic relationship between client and therapist, analysand and analyst, creates a unique togetherness that is usually not found outside of the therapeutic relationship. There are many factors which contribute to this special togetherness. The regular meetings, the lack of judgment, frequent self-disclosures and an open exploration of personal issues, all contribute in creating a special relationship. This togetherness, in and of itself, is part of the overall healing process.

These factors are usually lacking in non-therapeutic relationships. Even when they are manifest, they are usually interpreted as inappropriate for the situation or as signs of weakness and vulnerability.

This blatant dichotomy is strikingly apparent when a patient begins therapy and whenever resistances appear. When patients begin therapy, they usually feel somewhat uncomfortable in having the unique opportunity to share intimate details with another person. Statements such as "I have never told this to anyone before," "Can I trust you with the issue of confidentiality," "I feel so uneasy sharing my private thoughts," or "I am concerned that if I share this, you will not like me or you will think less of me," underlie how unaccustomed the client is in sharing secret thoughts and vulnerabilities. People usually want to project an image of niceness, friendship and helpfulness. They so desperately want to be liked and admired that they repress the shadow or "other side" completely. They project themselves as a complete rose garden without any thorns.

This process not only makes togetherness inaccessible, it even accentuates unique aspects of loneliness. The shadow parts become the exclusive possession of that lonely person.

The other extreme of this privacy is extreme openness, such as the inappropriate statements of some psychotic patients to everyone and at any time, made without utilizing common defense mechanisms.

What is needed in human relationships in life is a commitment to togetherness based on appropriate mutual sharing and this process can bridge the gap in which everyone finds oneself in complete isolation. People can then present themselves not as good, virtuous and religious, but rather as individuals who struggle with the basic issues of life, faith and doubt. Their struggles and challenges will not be repressed but acknowledged. The question of what is appropriate remains a dynamic challenge in the constantly changing circumstances. However, the commitment to loneliness and togetherness as belonging to the rhythm of living is a guide in itself.

A homiletical interpretation of a Biblical commandment expresses this commitment to togetherness in a beautiful way.

In reference to returning a lost item, the Bible states that you are not supposed to pretend that you had not seen the lost object (Deuteronomy 22:3). One needs to acknowledge that one has perceived a lost object. Rabbi Leo Baeck comments on this sentence in a most inspiring and beautiful way:

And a spirit is characterized not only by what it does

but, no less,

by what it permits,

what it forgives,

and what it beholds in silence. (on Corita Kent's painting)

One needs to acknowledge all aspects of oneself. Just as we must restore a lost object and not turn aside, every one of us is required to restore ourselves, to heighten our self-awareness and to acknowledge our dark side. We cannot ignore childhood emotional or sexual abuse or anything else about our specific history, past or present. Acknowledgement, awareness, and appropriate sharing with one another will create an atmosphere and ambience of togetherness. This togetherness will be a celebration. The celebration will acknowledge the frailties, struggles and challenges that everyone must encounter. When this is accomplished, one can recite Psalm 23 not only while lying on one's death bed, not only at a funeral, not only through difficult times in life, but as a celebration of a life which is lived to one's fullest potential.

"The Lord is my shepherd" - no one is lonely, either in life or in death. "He will restore my soul" - throughout life, a person will constantly search for the inner voices of the soul and be aware of all things, positive and negative. In that way, a person is a partner with God in life and in death.

References

Altmann, A. and Stern, S.M. (Eds.) (1958). Isaac Israeli: A Neoplatonic Philosopher of the Early Tenth Century. London: Oxford University Press.

Altmann, A. (1973). Moses Mendelssohn. Alabama: The University of Alabama Press.

Beck, A.T. and Beamesdorfer, A. (1974). "Assessment of Depression: The Depression Inventory," Psychological Measurement in Psychopharmacology. Pichot (Ed.). 2, pp. 151-169.

Erikson, E. (1968). Identity: Youth and Crisis. New York: W.W. Norton.

Fromm, E. (1963). The Art of Loving. New York: Bantam Books.

Fromm-Reichman, F. (1959). Psychoanalysis and Psychotherapy. Chicago: The University of Chicago Press.

HaLevi, Y. (11th Century) (1960). Kuzari. Ed. by Isaak Heinemann. Philadelphia: The Jewish Publication Society.

Hertz, J.H. (1981). The Pentateuch and Haftorahs. London: Soncino Press.

The Holy Scriptures (3 Vols.) (1982). Philadelphia: Jewish Publication Society.

Jung, C.G. (1933). Modern Man in Search of a Soul. New York: Harcourt Brace Jovanovich.

Kagan, Y.M.H. (1958). Sefer HaMitzvot HaKatzer. New York: Yeshiva Chofetz Chaim.

Lichtenstein, A. (1981). The Seven Laws of Noah. New York: The Rabbi Jacob Joseph School Press.

Maimonides, M. (12th Century) (1974). The Guide of the Perplexed. Translated by S. Pines. Chicago: The University of Chicago Press.

Maimonides, M. (12th Century) (1962). Mishneh Torah. (6 Vols.) New York: M.P. Press.

The Midrash (10 Vols.) (1961). H. Freeman and M. Simons (Eds.). London: Soncino Press.

Rosenberg, J. (1856), Kovetz Maase Yedai: Geonim Kadmonim. Berlin: Friedlandersche Buchdruckerei.

Soloveitchik, J.B. (1965). "The Lonely Man of Faith," Tradition. 1975, 7 (2).

Streisand, B. (1974). Being at War with each Other. New York:
Columbia.

The Talmud (18 Vols.) (1961). I. Epstein (Ed.). London:
Soncino Press.

Twersky, I. (1972). A Maimonides Reader. New York: Behrman
House, Inc.

Twersky, I. (1980). Introduction to the Code of Maimonides
(Mishneh Torah). Yale Judaica Series, Vol. XXII. New Haven
and London: Yale University Press.

PART III

On Suffering

CHAPTER 6

Coping with Suffering: Job, Judaism and Jung

Part I - Answer to Jung

The night after I contemplated applying to the analyst
training program at the Carl Gustav Jung Institute of Los
Angeles, I had a dream that I would write a book entitled
Answer to Jung, which would address Jung's major work on
theodicy entitled Answer to Job (1973). My thoughts regarding
entrance into the Jung Institute were also reflected in the
dream in that I have no desire to become a Jungian analyst.
Jung himself remarked that he would be appalled at the concept
of a "Jungian." I hope to use my association with the Jung
Institute to creatively select elements within the psycho-
spiritual framework that Jung established, and build on these
elements. This creativity will be free-flowing. It may confirm
some basic aspects of Jungian psychology, modify others, and
refute others. Thus, while the dream may superficially reflect
boldness and haughtiness, it actually represents apprehensive-
ness and trepidation.

I am not an expert on all of Jung's thoughts and ideas but
would like to critically examine some of Jung's basic assumptions regarding theodicy, and offer an alternative approach
from a psychological-Jewish perspective. My trepidation here
represents a guardedness in approaching another system that is
primarily rooted in Christian theology and historicity. Many
Christian scholars, including Jung, view world history and
thought as being a precursor or successor to what they perceive
as the central event of history -- i.e., the rise of Christianity. George Foot Moore, the distinguished Christian scholar
who wrote on normative Jewish theology, severely criticized his
colleagues who interpreted the history of the Second Jewish
Commonwealth as a precursor to the arrival of New Testament
theology (1921). I agree that the concept of a natural evolu-
tionary history of ideas is cogent and poignant. However, this
natural development of ideas, concepts, and thoughts needs to
be approached using an a priori methodology, without any pre-
conceived notion on the veracity of a religious doctrine.
Naturally, this approach is as valid for Judaism as it is for
Christianity.

While my very brief dream also implies that while I may or
may not be able to understand the issue of theodicy within a
total theological framework of Judaism, Jung's certainty can be
questioned and may ultimately be refuted. Despite the seriousness of the topic, both personally and theologically, the title
"Answer to Jung" in direct contrast to "Answer to Job" injects
a light and humorous note into an otherwise heavy and somber

96

topic. This was the mood of the dream as well. This combination of lightness and heaviness is also characteristic of God. The Talmud (Abodah Zarah 3b) describes God's activities to include studying Torah, matchmaking, and playing with Leviathan. God studies, explores, and thinks; God is interested in the happiness and stability of mankind and assists man and woman to find each other; and God plays, laughs, and has a sense of humor. Perhaps man, as he searches for meaning in his life, needs to combine these God-like elements of study, welfare, and playfulness. This process, therefore, is not destined to find an absolute answer to the issue of theodicy. Perhaps there is no one answer. Perhaps there are many and perhaps there are none. The search itself, however, already feels soothing. The process, the engagement with tradition in an open dialogue, is the reward. The Mishnah states: "The reward for the performance of a Divine commandment is the commandment itself" (Abot 4:2). The reward for engaging in this process is not some tentative goal, but genuine involvement in the activity.

The playfulness with Leviathan suggests that God is also involved with the issue of theodicy -- but in a light way. "Leviathan" has many connotations. It suggests the possibility of supernatural enemies of God, an ongoing battle between God and another God-like power (Psalms 74:13,14). Nevertheless this force - named Leviathan, personifying chaos and rebelliousness towards God - is interpreted as a playmate in the Talmud which describes God sporting and playing with Leviathan (Abodah Zarah 3b). This transformation of the Leviathan from adversary to playmate suggests multiple modalities for the issue of theodicy. As already mentioned, perhaps the approach toward the problem should incorporate playfulness and easiness rather than exclusively philosophical casuistry. The transformation of the Leviathan into a playmate demonstrates demonstrate that God is the victor over the other supernatural force. Or, perhaps, the victory is in the transformation itself -- to somehow change the antagonist into a necessary and helpful element in creation.

My title, however bold, is considerably less presumptuous than Jung's title. "Answer to Job" implies that God's response is inadequate and that Jung's response is superior to God's. "Answer to Jung" comes from a positive impulse in trying to understand God's word rather than from an antagonistic approach to God. I am making no a priori claim to being able to answer Job in a manner other than interpreting the book as it stands by itself.

The Book of Job is an important book included in the Bible. The issue as to why evil, pain, and suffering are part and parcel of man's life, and the theological implications of this truth cry out from the beginning of world history to the present. Philosophically, evil, pain, and suffering each connote a different idea. For our purposes, however, it is not necessary to differentiate between these various concepts. Let us understand the question in a Wittgensteinian sense (Wittgenstein, 1953, pp. 31-32). Were I to ask one hundred random people whether they have experienced evil, pain and suffering - there would be a unanimous positive response. This is the way I have conceptually defined the problem: not philosophically (whether or not evil, pain, and suffering exist ontologically) but rather, what does it mean experientially? The Talmud also relies on what the populace does and what they think. When there exists an unknown, the Talmud states: " Go and see what is the usage of the people" (Erubin 14b).

The existence of evil, pain, and suffering does not negate the beauty and exhilarating excitement of life. Many people feel moments of self-actualization and self-fulfillment in the act of helping one another; and the many moments of spiritual union with God and the cosmos are breathtaking. Equally rewarding is the enjoyment of various relationships, with their normal highs and lows of everyday life. The values and principles by which we ultimately try to improve the world for future generations are meaningful goals. The innumerable personal moments of contentment and the ineffable experiences of a very private nature are also part of everyone's experience. Despite the moments of joy, it is nonetheless true that evil, suffering and pain also prevail.

Part II - Analysis of God's Answer to Job

The issue of theodicy has perplexed mankind from the beginning of time. Its most poignant and literary form is the Book of Job. Every religion, philosophy, Biblical exegesis, and indeed every thoughtful person has attempted to reconcile the suffering of the righteous with the concept of Divine justice. The purpose of this paper is to compare and contrast salient medieval Jewish Biblical exegesis and Carl Gustav Jung's experiential reaction to the Book of Job.

Why? Why me? Why now? What is the meaning of punishment inflicted on a just individual? What is God doing and where is His justice? These are the central concerns of Job as well as the eternal inquiries of every human being.

Who is Job? What biographical data is available? Opinions in the Talmud and Midrash place Job either as a contemporary of Abraham or Moses or in the time of the Judges. The range of opinions includes the possibility that Job never existed (Talmud, Baba Batra 14b-16b). Perhaps the Rabbis are indicating that Job's situation transcends specific time and space,

98

that in reality Job's problem occurs in every era, to every person in different degrees. Another indication of the universality of the Job issue is Job's relationship to Judaism. Opinions range from his being a gentile, gentile prophet, or righteous proselyte, to his being a Jew (Talmud, Baba Batra 14b-16b). Job's religious denomination is irrelevant. His time in the history of the world is irrelevant. His suffering is representative of mankind and Divine justice is similarly a universal theological issue.

Jung approached the problem of evil from a world point of view. He confronted the reality of evil and doubts about the nature of the Divine image through his own experiences, encounters with his patients and the suffering of millions during World War II and the Holocaust. Jung's interpretation of the Book of Job differs markedly from that of some of the medieval Jewish Biblical commentators. Surprisingly, though, some of his statements find their parallels in Kabbalistic literature.

In order to understand these varying analyses of the Biblical tale, an a priori examination of the text itself is in order. Job is described as a pious and God-fearing person who not only obeys the letter of the law but also meticulously senses the spirit of the law. He is the epitome of a religious personality. A dialogue between God and Satan ensues. God is very proud of the devout Job. Satan claims that Job's devoutness is due to the fact that he has everything he desires. God and Satan agree to test Job to determine whether his piety is dependent on or independent of his welfare. Despite Job's steadfastness in the face of his initial trials and tribulations, he ultimately curses the day he was born. Chapters three through thirty-seven of the text describe the attempts of Elifaz, Bildad, Tzofer and Elihu to try to assuage Job's suffering by offering theological reasons for God's actions. Elifaz suggests that no man is without sin. Bildad reiterates the theologic truth that God is just. Tzofer castigates Job for his unrelenting questioning of God's justice. Job refuses to be consoled by any of these three friends or their arguments. The friends ultimately cease their dialogue with Job and recognize his righteousness. Elihu, a fourth friend, tries to convince Job of God's constant Divine providence. The last attempt is also futile from Job's perspective. God's response is equally problematic. God presents to Job His unfathomable wonders of creation and his marvels of nature. All of God's powers and deeds seem to imply that it is presumptuous of man to question God's justice or even to try to fathom his own suffering. Job acknowledges that he is of small account (Job 42:6) and that in view of God's unanswerable questions, he will proceed no further with his questioning of God's justice. Therefore, God's response to Job's suffering is basically an

99

emphatic statement that man cannot understand his fate and therefore should not even attempt to. Job's friends are rejected by God - implying that their view of suffering as proof of sin is not valid. The absence of any charge of guilt against Job in God's reply constitutes Divine vindication of Job's innocence.

What in fact is God's response to Job? It appears to be that man's cognizance of Divine powers should create within him an awareness that he is nothing but dust and ashes. With this perception of the relationship between himself and his Creator, man ceases to question God.

It is precisely with this unquestioning acceptance of Divine providence that the following discussion explores the question of the suffering of the righteous and the significance of God's response to Job.

The epilogue of the Book of Job tells of God's bestowing bountiful and limitless reward on Job. He is consoled about his previous misfortune and his current happy and blessed state exceeds every previous contentment. Through Job's maturation and new wisdom, God appears placated (Job 42:7) and Job appears to be in paradise already in "this world." However, this "happy ever after" epilogue does not obliterate nor diminish Job's previous state of suffering and pain.

The preceding objective summary of Job's story accentuates the primary episodes but fails to mention the underlying processes and metacommunication that transpire (Yankelovich and Barrett, 1971; Yalom, 1975). Process refers to "the relationship implication of interpersonal transactions" (Yalom, 1975). Metacommunication refers to the "communication about the communication ... a message about the nature of the relationship between the two interacting individuals" (Yalom, 1975).

There are three key processes that underlie God's relationship to man as demonstrated in the Book of Job. The first process is God's acceptance of Satan's challenge to test Job. What does this tell us about the image of God, if God accepts Satan's challenge and by so doing, causes unnecessary suffering to a righteous man? This is certainly not the first time that God tests people through painful events. God's test of Abraham involves inflicting excruciating mental anguish despite His change of instruction just before Abraham plans to sacrifice his son. Can the reader envision God responding in an alternative manner to Satan? God could have responded by saying "based on My omniscience I know that..." or "I do not accept your challenge since it causes undeserved pain to Job."

100

The second process is the manner of God's unique response to Job. Why does God choose the whirlwind as His medium to appear to a broken man? To appear as an omnipotent God seems reasonable before a mighty Samson, but there appears to be something incongruous in God's emphasizing His strength to such an afflicted man. In addition, does God's answer (man's inability to understand the ultimate justice of Divine reward and punishment) ameliorate Job's suffering or does it perhaps add to his pain? It seems that Job's response to God's answer is his own self-afflicting punishment by proclaiming that "I am dust and ashes" (Job 42:6). This total diminution of man seems antithetical to God's description of the creation of man as "in the image of God" (Genesis 1:27). And yet God accepts Job's acquiescence.

The third process is the final reward given to Job after his acquisition of the new knowledge, namely, that man cannot understand his fate. Job's reward is described as greater bliss than he had ever known before. This reference may serve as reassurance that ultimately man will experience earthly rewards if he recognizes that he is nothing in contrast to the Almighty or perhaps, if he has suffered unjustly.

Underlying all three processes is the fact that man's suffering need not spell isolation from God. The Divine revelation in the form of the whirlwind is itself an act of grace symbolizing that man has not been forsaken. It appears that God's presence is more than enough to sustain man. Job does not even interrupt God's speech to ask to be delivered from his suffering. Thus even when God closes His eyes, He still sees man.

There appear to be two conflicting interpretations to the issues raised in the story of Job. These two approaches differ as to whether it is possible that God can afflict man with undeserved suffering or whether God's justice is impeccable and man is responsible for everything that happens to him. Jung and the Zohar express the former opinion, while Rashi (Rabbi Solomon ben Isaac, 1040-1105) and Maimonides (1135-1204) adopt the latter opinion.

Jung emphasizes at the outset that his Answer to Job is his "subjective reaction of a modern man with a Christian education who comes to terms with the Divine darkness which is unveiled in the Book of Job" (Jung, 1973). In his subjective reaction, Jung does not try to respond via any intellectual tricks, but rather from the depth of his soul as it is affected by the violence inflicted upon Job.

The first process discussed above is addressed by Jung at the very beginning. How and why can God accept Satan's wager?

101

His acceptance reflects a God who decides not to act omnisciently, but rather in a fashion indicating a dark and evil side of His nature. Does not this imply a duality irreconcilable with our image of God's unity? Jung reconceptualizes God's unity as representing an antinomy - He is both a persecutor and a helper in one. When man requests God to help him, man is asking God to be an advocate against God Himself. In the Biblical story, God abandons his faithful servant to a Satanic spirit and allows Job to experience the depth of suffering. Why did not God act omnisciently? Jung suggests that perhaps God is jealous of man. Man has the ability, indeed the necessity, to reflect due to his limitations. God, however, being omnipotent, lacks the need to reflect on His actions. God is not responsible to a higher power. Therefore He has no need to reflect on Himself. Perhaps God's acquiescence to Satan is the result of His suspicion that man possesses a certain light (characteristic) that God Himself lacks (Kahn and Solomon, 1975). This inability to reflect on Himself determines His relations to His creations. God is dependent on people to assure Him that He is really there.

God's lack of self-reflection is certainly not any excuse for allowing Satan to take charge of Job. By killing Job's children, allowing bodily injury with premeditation, and denying the possibility of a fair trial, God intentionally violates at least three of His commandments.

Job's pain is intensified when his wife and "friends" try to explain to him the justifiable reasons for his situation. There is no demonstration of sympathetic participation of human understanding on their part. These seemingly wise friends seem totally lacking in any of the Carkhuff principles - warmth, empathy, genuineness, etc. (Traux and Carkhuff, 1967). Job's justified complaint finds no ear that is willing to listen. Job's inability to communicate and be heard and his friends' moralizing continue the Satanic play.

In the midst of his suffering and during the attempted consolation, Job reaches a new height in the man-God relationship. By realizing God's inner antinomy, Job experiences the numinous (Otto, 1967). By insisting on his innocence and standing his ground, Job creates a situation that forces God to reveal His true nature: "Who is this that darkens counsel by words without insight?" (Job 38:2).

Presumably God is rebuking Job. What has Job done? The only error he has committed is his insistence on Divine justice. God, however, never claims to be only just. He proudly proclaims might over right. Through God's speech, Job gains new insight into God and realizes the antinomy within God -

sometimes God demonstrates His "right" and sometimes His "might."

For 71 verses God describes His omnipotence to a person who is sitting in ashes and who has experienced Divine wrath at its harshest. God is hardly paying any attention to Job's real situation. This is true at the beginning, middle and end of the book. God initially ignores Job's righteousness, prolongs His wrath by presenting Job's unsympathetic friends, and ultimately confronts Job with His tremendous powers -- as if Job were not already aware of them. Why is God intentionally ignoring Job's situation? His constant emphasis on omnipotence makes little sense in relationship to Job. Jung suggests that Job serves as a continuing vehicle in God's discussion and wager with Satan. Why, then, is God interested in demonstrating verbal "might" in front of Satan? God realizes that somehow Satan beguiled Him into this wager. This shows weakness on His part. To offset this impression, God responds in a mighty fashion from the whirlwind.

Job realizes that God is not addressing him, but rather that God is involved with Himself. In order to eliminate Satan from the picture, God casts suspicion on Job as a man who demands justice, and then switches suddenly to a manifestation of unassailable power. Job, realizing what has taken place and noting that Divine justice has never been mentioned, transforms his adamant request into meek acquiescence. Recognizing the dark side of God, Job views himself as a pawn who has seen both the King's blunder and His attempt to rectify it. Job sees what even Moses did not see - more than the back of God! After Job's vision, he repents in dust and ashes. Formerly, the innocent Job viewed God as a "good" God, just and legally faithful to His covenant. Now he sees God as a Divine unconsciousness - therefore His actions are beyond moral judgment. Job has a new perception of God. Job has adjusted his understanding to enable his life to continue.

Jung concludes that God has a divided self. On the one hand, He regards human life and happiness without significance, yet He needs man for a partner to regard Him properly. Succinctly stated - He desires to be loved and praised as just, yet He acts with wrath and violates His moral code.

How does man react to such a God? Must we all be like Job in ultimately acquiescing and lavishing praise upon God?

Similar to Jung's conclusions are some of the interpretations offered by the Zohar, the classic work on the Kabbalah (Jewish mysticism). Job offers burnt offerings (Olot, Job 1:5), a type of sacrifice that is totally consumed and ascends to heaven. The Zohar interprets this episode as proof that Job

103

did not placate God's other side, Satan. Thus Job views God as a Being who is totally good. Being oblivious to God's other, evil side, Job is sentenced to be punished by God Himself in order to obtain a total picture of God in which good and evil are fused together.

This view of God is similar to Nahmanides' (Moses ben Nahman, 1194-1270) interpretation of the Temple service on the Day of Atonement (Leviticus 16:7,8). God instructs the high priest to prepare two rams: one for God and one for Azazel (Satan). This sacrifice to Azazel is basically an act of obeying and serving God, not Satan (Soloveitchik, 1974). Nahmanides cites the illustration of a king who tells his servant to feed or give money to a third party; thereby do we win the king's favor. The High Priest takes both sacrifices to the Tabernacle; both are gifts to God, and the lot decides which ram God wants us to send into the desert. Our fulfillment of this precept is solely to obey the will of God.

With this interpretation, the first process mentioned above becomes clarified. God accepts Satan's wager in order to placate him. For if man is negligent in his obligation to the other side, God must intervene and placate Satan.

Thus, both Jung and the Zohar suggest the possibility that God is a composite of good and evil. In Jung's interpretation, the antinomy is part of the unity of God, while in the Zohar it is manifested through Satan, whom God must always take care of.

At the other end of the spectrum are Rashi and Maimonides who claim that Job was in error and that God's justice is impeccable. These commentators, as well as others, ascribe to Job incomplete piety, though nowhere are Job's sins mentioned either explicitly or hinted at indirectly. Thus, Rashi and Maimonides appear to be more concerned with not altering their previous image of God than with reacting experientially to the tale as it is told. They prefer to see some righteousness of Job throughout the book and yet find reason to account for God's speech (Glatzer, 1966).

Rashi's Job has an imperfect but deep-seated fear of God. Many of Job's rebellious utterances are modified in Rashi's interpretation. In 9:13 and 9:16, Rashi changes Job's protests to statements of piety (also 9:20, "If I am righteous, my own mouth will condemn me," Rashi adds "fear of God will silence my voice."). Apparently Rashi approached the Book of Job in an a priori fashion. Not being able philosophically or theologically to visualize a protesting Job, despite precedents of Abraham and Moses, Rashi describes Job as a devout man. Yet, despite his fear of God, Job's piety was imperfect. He said that God "destroys the innocent and the wicked" (9:22). In addition,

104

Job was verbose and spoiled the Divine plan that God's Name should rest on he who is righteous and just, as described at the outset of the book. These and other imperfections are accentuated to justify God's speech (Chapter 38).

Maimonides (Guide, Part III, Chapters 22-23) claims that Job's deficiency was in his lack of wisdom. He points out that Job is described as ethical and upright, but no mention is made of his attainment of wisdom and intelligence. This lack of wisdom is demonstrated by his confusion in not comprehending his afflictions. Satan, noticing this deficiency in Job's intellectual development, instigates God's action. Lacking wisdom, knowing God only from tradition, and confused by his misfortune, Job views God as contemptuous of man. However, true human knowledge leads to a humble acknowledgement of the uniqueness and incomparability of Divine knowledge. It is this recognition that enables man to bear suffering and evil. This perception is what Job lacked before his trial. Intellectual maturity is attained once man has freed himself from the error of imagining God's knowledge to be similar to that of mankind. One can only wonder, why does God teach this truth experientially so frequently?

Maimonides' interpretation lends credence to a different understanding of God's address. God majestically ignores the issue as Job has posed it. Instead of giving an explanation for Job's suffering, God confronts him with a series of ironic questions intended to convince him of the insignificance of human knowledge and power. All this seems to imply that it is presumptuous of man to question God's justice. Having attained this new knowledge, Job recedes in humility, recognizing that he is but dust and ashes.

Maimonides' interpretation has some similarity to a well known story.

A father was teaching his little son to be less afraid, to have more courage, by having him jump down the stairs. He placed his boy on the second stair and said, "Jump, and I'll catch you." And the boy jumped. Then the father placed him on the third step, saying, "Jump, and I'll catch you." Though the boy was afraid, he trusted his father, did what he was told and jumped into his father's arms. Then the father put him on the next step, and then the next step, each time telling him, "Jump and I'll catch you," and each time the boy jumped and was caught by his father. And so this went on. Then the boy jumped from a very high step, just as before; but this time the father stepped back, and the boy fell flat on his face. As he picked himself up, bleeding and crying, the father said to

105

him, "That will teach you: never trust anyone, even your father." (story has been adapted, Hillman, 1964)

Is this the best educational method to accomplish the desired goals? Could not the father and The Father have thought of alternative ways?

Rashi and Maimonides agree that Job was in error. Rashi's emphasis is on Job's imperfect piety, while Maimonides stresses Job's lack of wisdom in comprehending the uniqueness of God's knowledge. The similar approaches of Rashi and Maimonides are in direct contrast to the contrary viewpoints of Jung and the Zohar.

The Book of Job is extremely complex. I have offered two opposing interpretations to the problems of God's image and man's worldly experiences.

There is another side to this problem. Why doesn't man ask, "Why do I have it so well?" Why does one question God's justice when experiencing discomfort and not inquire about God's bountiful mercy when experiencing contentment? Do people not see God in their joys?

The issue of theodicy and the suffering of the righteous has no "answer." Each person will confront this issue either vicariously or directly in his or her lifetime. Man's experiential reaction to this phenomenon will create and form his image of God, which is a psychic truth (Jung, 1973). A psychic truth can not be explained nor proven empirically in any physical way. Since this issue is not in the realm of a physical truth, man's psyche will continue to comment upon and struggle with the image of God.

Are there any practical manifestations to one's image of God? I believe so. The image of God that allows for the possibility of undeserved suffering enables one to cope with the world experientially. It allows for one to believe in God, yet witness the birth of a crippled child, natural catastrophes that sweep away thousands, and the millenia of historical suffering.

References

Friedman, T. (1971). Encyclopaedia Judacia, volume 10. New York: The Macmillan Company.

Glatzer, N. (1966). "The Book of Job and Its Interpreters," Biblical Motifs. Edited by A. Altmann. Cambridge, Mass.: Harvard University Press.

Hillman, J. (1964). "Betrayal," The Guild of Pastoral Psychology, Guild Lecture No. 128. Los Angeles: Analytical Psychology Club.

Jung, C.G. (1973). Answer to Job. Princeton: Princeton University Press.

Kahn, I. and Solomon, H. (1975). Job's Illness: Loss, Grief and Interaction. New York: Pergamon Press.

Maimonides, M. (12th century) (1974). The Guide of the Perplexed. Chicago: The University of Chicago Press.

Mishnah (1961). I. Epstein (Ed.). London: Soncino Press.

Moore, G.F. (1921). "Christian Writers on Judaism," Harvard Theological Review. Volume 14 (3).

Otto, R. (1967). The Idea of the Holy. New York: Oxford University Press.

Soloveitchik, J.B. (1974). "The Enormous Chesed of Hashem on Yom Kippur," New York: Rabbinical Council of America.

Talmud. (1961). I. Epstein (Ed.). London: Soncino Press.

The Holy Scriptures (1985). Philadelphia: Jewish Publication Society.

Truax, C.B, and Carkhuff, R.R. (1967). Toward Effective Counseling and Psychotherapy: Training and Practice. Chicago: Aldine Publishing Co.

Wiesel, E. (1975). Messengers of God. New York: Random House.

Wittgenstein, L. (1953). Philosophical Investigations. Oxford: Basil Blackwell.

Yalom, I. (1975). The Theory and Practice of Group Psychotherapy. New York: Basic Books.

Yankelovich, D., and Barrett, W. (1971). Ego and Instinct. New York: Vintage Books.

Zohar. (1984). London: Soncino Press.

CHAPTER 7

Quality of Life

"Though the physicality of death destroys an individual,
the idea of death can save him (Yalom, 1980)." An awareness of
death moves one away from trivial preoccupations and concerns
and provides life with depth and substance from an entirely
different perspective.

An awareness of the importance of medical ethics allows
physicians and their patients to focus on the most profound and
pressing issues relating to the preservation of life. Though
the issues of medical ethics may appear very complex, remote,
and esoteric, their real-life application is a vital, everyday
part of modern medical treatment. Indeed, both the quality and
quantity of life are at the root of medical ethics.

Quantity of life is defined as the duration of one's
existence. But what are the parameters and criteria of quality
of life? In the realm of medical ethics, this is the quintessential area of investigation. Physicians, bioethicists,
attorneys, and clergy have not ventured into this realm in a
methodological manner. They have arrived at their conclusions
from a subjective and personal stance. Frequently, the profes-
sionals have been guided by "situational ethics," i.e., doing
what appears appropriate in a particular situation under particular circumstances.

Nowhere are the ethical dilemmas involving the quality of
life more pressing than with respect to death and dying. A
terminal cancer patient who is experiencing great pain suffers
cardiac arrest; should the patient be resuscitated? A family
member with a life-threatening illness refuses to undergo
treatment; should treatment be administered in violation of the
patient's expressed wishes?

The triumphs of modern medicine are everywhere. Achievements such as open-heart surgery and organ transplants, dialy-
sis machines that substitute for the kidneys, pacemakers that
regulate the beating of the heart, and vaccines that have made
once-dreaded diseases almost forgotten words have become com-
monplace. The new technologies do not always cure, but sometimes merely prolong the dying process. The irony of modern
medicine is that with the new technologies that vastly expand
the range of the possible has also come the anguish of deciding
when it is appropriate to use those capabilities.

The Indignity of 'Death with Dignity'

In trying to grapple with these most difficult issues, some
108

ethicists have introduced phrases such as "death with dignity." These proponents have intentionally used a phrase that evokes compassion and empathy. Paul Ramsey (1974) accentuates the absurdity of the phrase by entitling his article "The Indignity of 'Death with Dignity'". In contrast to "death with dignity" is Dylan Thomas's (1953) "Do Not Go Gentle into That Good Night", where he wrote "old age should burn and rage at the close of day; rage rage against the dying of the light."

"Death with dignity" is ultimately a contradiction in terms. Disease, injury, and congenital defects are --like death-- a part of life. Yet there is no campaign for accepting those things with dignity. Nor is there emphasis on "suffering with dignity." All of these occurrences, including death, are enemies and violations of human nobility. Grief over death, as well as the biopsychosocial pain of dying, need to be acknowledged.

Rabbi Soloveitchik's Views on Death

The antithetical relationship of death to life is reflected in the thought of Rabbi Joseph Soloveitchik (1983).

We have stated that Judaism, as reflected in the Halakhah, has a negative attitude toward death. A person is obligated to rend his garment and mourn for his relative. The Halakhah has established certain units of time with regard to mourning: the first day (on which mourning, according to many rishonim [early medieval authorities], is a biblical commandment), seven days, thirty days, twelve months. The onen, a mourner on the day of death, is forbidden to eat any sacred offerings; moreover the mourner does not have any sacrifices offered up on his behalf during the entire seven-day mourning period. The high priest is forbidden to let his hair grow and rend his garment for his dead relative, for preoccupation with the memory of the dead desecrates the holiness of the Temple and that of the high priesthood. Indeed many rishonim exempted the high priest from all rites of mourning. Holiness is rooted and embedded in joy. "And ye shall rejoice before the Lord your God seven days" (Lev.23:40), "and thou shalt rejoice in all the good" (Deut. 26:40), "and thou shalt be altogether joyful" (Deut. 16:15). Joy is the symbol of the real life in which the Halakhah is actualized. Avelut, mourning, and aninut, grief, however, are interwoven and bound up with that arch-opponent of holiness - death. Death and holiness constitute two contradictory verses, as it were, and the third harmonizing verse has yet to make its appearance. The Gaon of

109

Vilna, R. Joseph Dov Soloveitchik, his son, R. Hayyim, his grandson, R. Moses, R. Elijah Pruzna (Feinstein) never visited cemeteries and never prostrated themselves upon the graves of their ancestors. The memory of death would have distracted them from their intensive efforts to study the Torah.

It is only against this background that we can comprehend a peculiar feature in the character of many great Jewish scholars and Halakhic giants: the fear of death. Halakhic man is afraid of death; the dread of dissolution oftentimes seizes hold of him. My uncle, R. Meir Berlin (Bar-Ilan), related the following incident to me. Once he and R. Hayyim of Brisk happened to be staying in the same hotel in Libau on the shore of the Baltic. One fine, clear morning he arose at sunrise and went out on the balcony there to find R. Hayyim sitting - his head between his hands, his glance fixed upon the rays of the rising sun, entirely absorbed in the aesthetic experience of such a glorious cosmic spectacle and, at the same time, entirely bent beneath the oppressive weight of a soul-shattering melancholy and a black despair.

R. Berlin took hold of R. Hayyim's shoulder and shook it: "Why are you so troubled and disturbed, my master and teacher? Is something in particular responsible for your distress?"

"Yes," replied R. Hayyim, "I am reflecting upon the end of every man - death."

Halakhic man enjoyed the splendor of sunrise in the east and the swelling sea in the west, but this very experience, which contained in miniature the beauty of the cosmos as a whole and the joy of sheer existence, precipitated in him despair and deep depression. The beauty and splendor of the world on the one hand, and the fate of man, who can enjoy this mysterious magnificence for only a brief, fleeting moment, on the other hand, touched the chords of his sensitive heart, which sensed the entire tragedy concealed with this phenomenon: a great and resplendent world and man, "few of days, and full of trouble" (Job 14:1). The fear of death is transformed here into a quiet anguish, a silent pain, and a tender and delicate sadness that are adorned with the precious embellishment of a profound and lofty aesthetic experience. However, the individual who undergoes such an exalted experience is not the type who longs for transcendence, yearning to break out of the realm of the

110

concrete, for why should such a one be disheartened and grieved on account of the beauty of this world, which is but a pale reflection of a hidden, supernal existence. The Halakhic man who gazed at the first rays of the sun and reflected upon the beauty of the world and the nothingness of man in an ecstatic mood of joy intermixed with tragedy is a this-worldly man, an individual given over to concrete reality, who communicates with his Creator, not beyond the bounds of finitude, not in a holy, transcendent realm enwrapped in mystery, but rather in the very midst of the world and the fullness thereof.

"I said: I shall not see the Lord, even the Lord in the land of the living, etc. For the nether-world cannot praise Thee: death cannot celebrate Thee: they that go down into the pit cannot hope for Thy truth. The living, the living, he shall praise Thee, as I do this day; the Father to the children shall make known Thy truth" (Isa. 38:11-19), sang King Hezekiah when he recovered from his illness. "I shall not die, but live, and declare the works of the Lord" (Ps. 118:17), pleaded David, king of Israel, before his Creator. And the echo of these hymns still resounds through the world of Halakhah. (pp. 35-37)

Suffering

The proponents of "death with dignity" also invoke the concern of ameliorating the suffering of the dying patient.

The nature of suffering is a highly complex issue involving the individual's subjective pain-threshold and the value/meaning that is attached to the suffering (Meier, 1981). Marcel (1950), a French existentialist, stated that "life is not a problem to be solved but rather a challenge to be lived." Rabbi Soloveitchik (1983), a religious existentialist, stated that "against my will I was created and against my will I shall die, but through my will I shall live." These two highly eloquent and succinct statements reflect an alternative approach to a dying man's excruciating suffering.

It is not uncommon for suffering to occur not only during the course of a disease but also as a result of its treatment. A cancer patient may seek relief through chemotherapy and radiation treatment. Even when these treatments are successful, the success sometimes brings with it terrible side effects that some patients claim are equal to the disease itself. Medical science presumes the Cartesian dualism of mind and body. Yet suffering is experienced by persons. The understanding of the place of the person in human illness requires a

111

rejection of the historical dualism of mind and body. As long as the mind-body dichotomy is accepted, suffering is either subjective, and therefore not truly "real" - not within medicine's domain - or identified exclusively with bodily pain (Cassell, 1982). This distortion is itself an additional source of suffering.

The personal meaning which is identified with an illness affects the suffering of the patient. Rabbi Meier (1981) differentiated between the suffering of a patient with a chronic illness and a terminally ill patient. Phenomenologically and existentially, a patient with a chronic ailment perceives his future suffering in the present. Van den Berg (1972) explains man's relationship to time by theorizing that future and past are embodied in the present. Van den Berg states "The past is within the present: What WAS is the way it is appearing NOW. The future: what comes, the way it is meeting us now." A patient with a chronic ailment experiences not only present suffering, but also future anticipated suffering embodied in the present moment.

In contrast, a patient who is terminal experiences subjective death now, but not "eternal suffering." This experience of finiteness may motivate the patient to grow as a person and/or to achieve closure with his family and others with whom he has significant relationships. Even if this experience of finiteness brings depression, the patient knows that this depression is also finite and of temporary duration.

Therefore, wherever possible, suffering should be avoided or eliminated through medical care. But suffering should not be terminated by either "death with dignity," or a "good death" (euthanasia).

Viktor Frankl (1983) stated that the concept of death gives meaning to life. How can there be any meaning to life in the face of the fundamental transitoriness of existence? The idea of death does not eliminate the meaning of life, but - on the contrary - enhances the meaning of life. If life were infinite, then everything could be delayed ad infinitum. Only under the pressure of the transitoriness of existence is one required to act immediately. It is only the potentialities that are passing. Once a possibility has been actualized, it exists forever. The past contains not only past experiences but also the sufferings courageously lived through.

When reflecting on one's life, a person tends to dwell on his misgivings and fears, and forgets to look at the grandeur of the past. There is no need to pity an old man because life is behind him; on the contrary, one would have to envy him. While young men have only possibilities before them, old people

112

have their realities, which have already been actualized.

Frankl stated (1983) that life is meaningful in an unconditional sense, even under the most miserable conditions. Just
as there is an unconditional meaningfulness to life, there is
also an unconditional value to man. This unconditional value,
or dignity, does not depend on any "usefulness" in terms of
societal, family or individual functions. Real dignity,
including that of old or chronically sick people, relies on the
values with which they have lived and on the meanings they have
deposited into their personal pasts. This dignity cannot be
deleted. Those who do not ascribe this unconditional value to
old people, handicapped people and senile people would have
justified Hilter's euthanasia program of eliminating psychotic
people. It is only this unconditional value of every person
that restrains us from euthanasia activities.

"D equals S minus M," is Dr. Frankl's equation. Despair is
suffering without meaning. If a person is unable to remove the
current suffering, then one is mandated to try to impose a
meaning upon suffering. Nobody can give meaning; one has to
find meaning. Each and every individual may arrive at his or
her own meaning.

It has been said that if a doctor treats two cases in the
same way, then he has mistreated at least one of them. Everyone must find his own uniqueness to his situation. Doctors
cannot prescribe meaning to a patient suffering from meaninglessness. Doctors can describe the process of what is going on
in an individual in a given situation. The only thing doctors
can do is to study the lives of people who seem to have found
their 'answers' as against those who have not.

The discovery of meaning in a life situation can be arrived
at by three principal avenues. First, by doing something of
creative value. Secondly, by experiencing something beautiful -
through valuable research, scientific work, or through love.
The third avenue is the most courageous. One may still find
meaning precisely when confronted with a hopeless situation
that cannot be changed. It is in this type of situation that a
helpless victim has his greatest opportunity. He has the
capacity to turn a tragedy into a personal triumph and
accomplishment.

Dr. Frankl (1983) shared a moving story that exemplified
how one can rise above oneself. A few years after World War
II, a doctor examined a Jewish woman who wore a bracelet made
of baby teeth, mounted in gold. A beautiful bracelet, the
doctor remarked. Yes, the woman answered; you see, this tooth
here belongs to Miriam, this one to Esther and this one to
Samuel. She mentioned the names of her daughters and son,

according to their age; nine children, she added, and all of them had been taken to the gas chambers. Shocked, the doctor asked, "How can you live with such a bracelet?" Quietly, the Jewish woman replied, "I'm now in charge of an orphanage in Israel." Life is always a time of unparalleled potential for personal and interpersonal growth.

A Quest for Meaning

Whatever solution is suggested in the various ethical dilemmas which are presented, the approach must be in consonance with the basic meaning of life which the patient has developed. There have been various theistic and atheistic approaches to this most basic issue (Yalom, 1980).

A common theme exemplifying a Jewish attitude to medical crises and ethical dilemmas is _engagement_ in value-oriented activities. Man is required to take a leap into commitment and action. Meaning must be pursued obliquely. A sense of meaningfulness is a by-product of engagement.

Wholehearted engagement enhances the possibility of one's completing the patterning of the events of one's life in some coherent fashion. A beautiful and moving Talmudic anecdote demonstrates how engagement in the last moment of a person's life can give meaning to suffering. One version of this incident is:

> Rabbi Hanina ben Teradyon was wrapped in the Torah from which he had been teaching and placed on a pyre of green brushwood, and his chest was drenched with water to prolong the agony. His disciples, watching the flames dancing over their beloved teacher, asked: " Master, what do you see?" He replied: "I see parchment burning, while the letters of the Torah soar upward." His disciples then advised him to open his mouth that the fire might enter and the sooner put an end to his suffering; but he refused to do so, saying: "it is best that He who has given life should also take it away; no one may hasten his own death." The executioner removed the wet sponge and fanned the flame, thus accelerating the end, and then plunged himself into the fire (Birnbaum, 1951).

The complete text of this story is found in the Talmud (Abodah Zarah 18a).

On their return, the Roman officials found Rabbi Hanina ben Teradyon sitting and occupying himself with the Torah, publicly gathering assemblies, and keeping the scroll of the Law in his bosom. Straightaway they took hold of him,

114

wrapped him in the Scroll of the Law, placed bundles of branches round him and set them on fire. They then brought tufts of wool, which they soaked in water, and placed them over his heart, so that he should not expire quickly. His daughter exclaimed, "Father that I should see you in this state!" He replied, "If it were I alone being burnt it would have been a thing hard to bear; but now that I am burning together with the Scroll of the Law, He who will have regard for the plight of the Torah will also have regard for my plight." His disciples called out, "Rabbi, what do you see?' He answered them, "The parchments are being burnt but the letters are soaring on high." "Open then your mouth so that the fire may enter into you." He replied, "Let Him who gave my soul take it away, but no one should injure oneself." The executioner then said to him, "Rabbi, if I raise the flame and take away the tufts of wool from over your heart, will you cause me to enter into the life to come?" "Yes, he replied." "Then swear unto me!" He swore unto him. He thereupon raised the flame and removed the tufts of wool from over his heart, and his soul departed speedily. The executioner then jumped and threw himself into the fire. And a heavenly voice exclaimed: Rabbi Hanina ben Teradyon and the executioner have been assigned to the world to come.

This very moving episode shows that any deliberate acceleration of the final release is prohibited, as exemplified by the martyred sage. Rabbi Hanina ben Teradyon, while being burnt at the stake by the Romans, refused to follow his disciples' advice to open his mouth to the flames in order to speed his death. Jewish law emphasizes the mitigation of a patient's suffering, especially in the ordeal prior to death, except at the cost of life itself. Judaism teaches that human life has infinite value (Jakobovits, 1975).

Rabbi Hanina's actions demonstrate that even one second before he became immortal, he achieved 'temporal immortality' by having engaged in valued activities. Once again, he assumed his role as a teacher of Torah. This time it was not only by didactic methodology but also by example. He taught the quintessential lesson of Jewish medical ethics: life has infinite value. Even in the excruciating suffering of a terminally ill person, meaning can be found by engaging in immortal lessons for mankind. Through man's awareness of his finitude and precisely because of it, man can achieve "infinite immortality." Once he is deceased, man's life is not something of the distant past but of the everlasting example for future generations. Rabbi Hanina's teachings are immortal.

References

Birnbaum, P. (1951). High Holyday Prayer Book. New York: Hebrew Publishing Company.

Cassell, E.J. (1982). "The Nature of Suffering and the Goals of Medicine," The New England Journal of Medicine. 306, (11).

Frankl, V.E. (1983). The Meaning of Suffering. Videocassette. Health Science Information Center, Cedars-Sinai Medical Center.

Jakobovits, I. (1975). Jewish Medical Ethics. New York: Bloch Publishing Company.

Marcel, G. (1950). The Mystery of Being. Chicago: Regnery.

Meier, L. (1981). Chronic Pain, Suffering, and Spirituality: The Relationship Between Chronic Pain, Suffering, and Different Religious Approaches. Unpublished Dissertation, University of Southern California.

Ramsey, P. (1974). "The Indignity of 'Death with Dignity,'" Hasting Center Studies, 2, (2).

Soloveitchik, J.B. (1983). Halakhic Man. (L. Kaplan, trans.). Philadelphia: The Jewish Publication Society of America.

Talmud (1961). I. Epstein (Ed.). London: Soncino Press.

Thomas, D. (1953). The Collected Poems of Dylan Thomas. New York: New Directions.

Van den Berg, J.H. (1972). A Different Existence. Pittsburgh: Duquesne University Press.

Yalom, I.D. (1980). Existential Psychotherapy. New York: Basic Books.

PART IV

On Life and Death

CHAPTER 8

Does Death Confer Meaning on Life? A Psycho-Biblical Approach

Life and the Dying Process

The psycho-<u>Halakhic</u> person of conscience is constantly aware of the finiteness of life, which includes not only the fact that a person is finite but also all the components of this process of finiteness. The two central components, prior to a person's death, are aging and illness. Thus, the awareness of the finiteness of life is in reality the cognizance that the dying process begins with birth. The Rabbis expressed this idea very succinctly by stating: "Rabbi Eliezer said: repent one day before your death" (Mishnah, Abot 2:10), on which the Talmud comments:

> Rabbi Eliezer's disciples asked him, 'Does a man know when he is going to die?' He said to them, 'Then certainly he should repent today, because maybe he will die tomorrow. Therefore, man should always be in the process of repenting.' (Talmud, Shabbat 153a)

The Talmud and Maimonides (Mishneh Torah, Teshubah 7:2) refer to King Solomon's statement that "your garments should always be white" (Ecclesiastes 9:8) as an illustration that one should always be prepared to stand before the Creator in as pure a state as possible. Thus, even when one is healthy, one can and should be aware that life is finite. A terminal illness only accentuates the reality and imminence of death and focuses more acutely on the duration of time left before one dies. The dying process begins at birth. Thus, "life" and the "dying process" are really parallel processes which take place during the same time-frame.

Sensitivity toward the finiteness of "life" and the synonymous "dying process" could easily lead to total preoccupation with morbidity, mortality, and suicide. Indeed the difference between healthy and neurotic preoccupation with death is often a matter of degree. A neurotic obsession with death may ultimately bring one to a state of total emotional immobility. A healthy awareness of life's finiteness constantly leads one to search for a meaningful existence.

Another way to approach the preoccupation with death is through denial. By denying the inevitable, life passes by. A classic example of denial is the situation in which a loved one has just died and the surviving spouse laments the fact that there was so much more to converse about. Yet, the couple had been married for many years. What were they waiting for? Or, are some emotions so difficult to articulate that they are

119

suppressed forever?

As with any state of mind, the frequency, duration, and intensity are the factors determining a healthy or unhealthy activity. Ultimately, these variables help to achieve stability in life. If any of these factors are out of proportion, the equilibrium can be upset.

In the many lectures and seminars that I give in the field of gerontology, I frequently begin with the following question. If medical science discovers a pill that would ensure longevity for 150 years, how many of you would want to take such a pill? Inevitably, the overwhelming response is to decline such an offer. Members of the audience generally explain that if we could be assured of maintaining our health, it could be a blessing. However, if longevity entails constantly declining health leading to lack of self-control and dependence on others, people usually gracefully decline the offer. Their responses are conceptually similar to the statement that life means health, stability, roses, motherhood, and baseball. When life, partially or totally, precludes these aspects, death is preferred. Such well intentioned people have not equated "life" with the "dying process." It is precisely this equation that allows one to find meaning in life.

If there were no death, there would also be no illness or aging. Succinctly stated, without death there would be no life.

Hillel stated: "If I am not for myself, who am I? If I am only for myself, what am I? And if not now, then when?" (Mishnah, Abot 1:14). These three statements are not three distinct thoughts, but represent one united idea. The fact that there may not be a tomorrow focuses attention on the here-and-now. There needs to be a balance between the development of self and altruistic behavior. If there were no death, there would be no dying, there would be no aging, there would be no illness, and there would be no life.

The Torah states the reason why life is finite. The Torah states: "And God said: My spirit shall not be in man forever, since he is also composed of flesh; and his days shall be one hundred and twenty years" (Genesis 6:3). God specifically created human beings with diametrically opposed entities, spirit and flesh, which cannot coexist eternally. Thus, God created people so that they would ultimately die. Death would then be a natural outgrowth of the lack of compatibility of flesh and spirit. If death is the natural outcome of life, death can be perceived without the value judgment of good or bad. Yet, prima facie, it appears from the Torah that death comes as a result of not listening to God's commandments.

120

And the Lord God commanded man, saying: of every tree of the garden you may surely eat; however, of the Tree o⁻ ₋nowledge of Good and Evil, you shall not eat, for in the day that you eat from it, you shall surely die. (Genesis 2:16,17)

God enjoins man to enjoy all the fruits and vegetables in the Garden of Eden with the exception of the Tree of Knowledge of Good and Evil. If man violates this singular commandment, his punishment is death. Thus, death appears to be not a natural outcome of "life" but part of an overall plan of reward and punishment.

Yet, this is obviously an oversimplification of the episode. First, what is the nature of this commandment? What does this commandment represent symbolically? Why is the punishment ascribed to the violation as severe as death? And finally, the question of questions: the majority of children and adults usually eat "forbidden fruit." When a parent says to a child you can play with every toy except toy x, inevitably the child will play with toy x. Did God want man to violate the first commandment so that man and not God would bring death into the world? Did God not want to be identified with death? And, more significantly, what is the relationship between God and man? Does God need man? Does man need God? Is the relationship reciprocal?

Having raised some central questions of theology and philosophy, let us look at one aspect of the creation story. On every day of creation, with the exception of the second day, the Torah states: "And God saw that it was 'good'" (Genesis 1:4, 1:10, 1:12, 1:18, 1:21). Upon the completion of the sixth day of creation, the Torah states: "And God saw all that was created and it was 'very good'" (Genesis 1:31). The other place in the Torah in which a variation of "very good" appears is in reference to the land of Israel. The Torah says: "The land which we passed through to explore it, is a 'very, very good' land" (Numbers 14:7). Thus, the Torah uses three gradations referring to the value judgment of good. If something is "good," it is not "very good," and if it is "very good," it is not "very, very good." The "very good" at the completion of the creation may refer to the interrelatedness of all the different and distinct parts of creation. This may be quite similar to the comments of an architect on a building he is designing. After completing the walls, windows, and roof, he may look at it with personal satisfaction. When he adds wallpaper and paint wherever appropriate, he proclaims with pride "it is good." Finally, when people move in and create ambience, atmosphere and a sense of domestication, he may proclaim with a smile "this is very good." The "very good" expressed by God

121

expresses pride and satisfaction, not only in every aspect of the process of creation, but also in the gestalt of the creation. Harmony and the interrelatedness of creation constituted the final creative act and this was declared as being "very good."

A word which is not used regarding creation is mushlam (complete) or tamim (whole), both having the connotation of perfection. Thus, creation is described with the adjective "very good," but not "very, very good," and not with any word connoting perfection. The creation of the world and the creation of man within this world is very good, but not perfect.

The second day of creation lacks the description of "good." Why? Rashi explains that the double description of good on the third day refers to the second and third day of creation (Genesis 1:7). However, the Zohar comments that on the second day of creation, God divided between the upper and lower waters and any process of division cannot be called "good" (Zohar, Genesis 1:7). Thus, the majority of creation was described as good; the second day lacked any positive descriptive statement, and upon the completion of creation it was declared "very good." God, a perfect Being by definition, created a world that was "very good."

The Torah states: "God blessed the seventh day and sanctified it by ceasing from all His work, which God had created to do" (Genesis 2:3). The Midrash asks what is meant by the phrase "created to do." The Midrash replies that it means that God created the world with much more left to do; having created man, the creation will continuously be completed by man (Kasher, 1944, 192-193). Therefore, man is considered as a partner with God in constantly completing the creation process. Nature is not sovereign; it is in service of man. Man needs to be in control of nature and not be controlled by it.

Indeed the Torah states: "...and God said to them (man and woman), be fruitful and multiply and inhabit the land and conquer (control) it" (Genesis 1:28). Man's primary task, qua human being, is to control and conquer nature. Thereby, he becomes a partner with God. God decided to create the world and ask man to be a partner with Him in the continuing process of creation.

Death was created by God when he created man. Death was never meant to be a punishment. The Torah states that God intentionally created man with two entities that cannot coexist forever - flesh and spirit. Indeed, not only is death not a punishment, but the Midrash understands it as something natural and "very good."

122

The Midrash comments on: "And God saw all that He had made and behold it was 'very good'" (Genesis 1:31) that "very good" refers to death (Midrash Rabbah, Genesis 9:5). Yes, even death was perceived as being part of the "very good" of the totality of creation.

We have tentatively concluded that:
1) the creation is "good" and "very good " but not perfect,
2) God created death by creating life and declared both to be part of the "very good" of the creation,
3) man is a partner with God in the continuous process of creation,
4) God created man with two diametrically opposed entities that cannot coexist forever - ipso facto, death, and
5) death assists man in living a life of meaning.

We are nevertheless left with the question, why does it appear that death is a punishment if in reality it is a natural process of life? If death is an inevitable consequence of life, why does the Torah introduce death as a result of not listening to God?

If death is a natural process of life and even part of the "very good" scheme of creation, what is the rationale for associating death with punishment for Adam and Eve's not listening to God. In order to deal with this central issue, let us turn our focus on the issue of what is a timely death, what is a premature death, what is a good death, and what is not a good death. What is the symbolism of living seventy or eighty or one-hundred-twenty years?

Life Fulfillment and Self-Actualization

The Torah describes the death of Abraham, Isaac, and King David in terms of life fulfillment and self-actualization. The Torah says: "Then Abraham expired, and died in a good old age, an old man, and full of years; and was gathered to his people" (Genesis 25:8); "And Isaac expired and he died and was gathered to his people an old man and full of days....."(Genesis 35:29); "And he (King David) died in good old age, full of days, riches and honor....."(Chronicles 1, 29:28). Nahmanides comments on the expressions "full days" and "full years;" "He witnessed the fulfillment of all the desires of his heart and was sated with all good things..... which means that his soul was sated with days, and he had no desire that the future days should bring something new" (Genesis 25:8).

The central theme of dying at a good old age is having lived a full life. Death as the completion of life could rightly be called a "natural" death.

123

There are innumerable examples of self-actualized people who died young (Rabbi Isaac Luria, Mozart); and many people who reach old age without even actualizing a small fraction of their potential. On tombstones the least significant information is inscribed: the year of birth and the year of death. Life is not measured or evaluated by length but by fulfillment of one's potential. The awareness of death should intensify the awareness of life. The knowledge of one's finiteness should awaken the person toward self-actualization, creativity, and sensitivity to the here-and-now. Man knows that he is mortal and that death is inevitable. Man acknowledges the death of others; but he detaches this knowledge from himself. To live life to the fullest requires full acknowledgement of one's mortality. This full acknowledgement of our finiteness intensifies the awareness of life. Life allows only a limited amount of time. Death and the full acknowledgement of our finiteness intensifies the awareness of life. Death and the full acknowledgement of one's mortality is a positive force toward the realization of unique talents and desires. When man actualizes his unique potentiality, he experiences self-fulfillment. At that point, life is complete and death has served the most positive force of life.

Seven years ago I led a discussion group at a conference dealing with death and dying. The entire group had listened to presentations from a rabbi, a psychologist, a social worker, a physician, and from a terminally ill patient. In my small group discussion, everyone expressed how courageous the terminally ill patient was since she was dying; however, the group denied the fact that they were all dying. In reality, the terminally ill patient was living life to her fullest. Our attitude toward death is inextricably intertwined with time perspective. The major difference between the terminally ill patient and the other participants was that the patient was acutely aware that her days were numbered, whereas the others denied the fact that all our days are numbered. What is necessary is to experience life as unlimited potential meaningfulness and self-actualization while one is still in the midst of it. Then when one has lived, one can die. Then death serves as the natural completion of one's life.

Death is Certain; the Time of Death is Not.

The Torah states that man's years are one-hundred-and-twenty years (Genesis 6:3). The Psalmist proclaims: "The length of our life is seventy years, or, by reason of strength, eighty years" (Psalms 90:10). Rabbinic literature describes appropriate norms starting from age five until one hundred years. Sixty years is considered "young old" and seventy years is old! It is assumed that reaching eighty years is due to extraordinary strength! Ninety is characteristic of a bent-over old,

124

old person. One who reaches a hundred years is considered functionally dead (Mishnah, Abot 5:21). Naturally, all these ages are average ages. Thus, the Bible and Rabbinic literature indicate various age-appropriate norms that one passes through in one's lifetime. From this discussion it appears that various ages are indeed considered a timely death. It appears that any age above sixty years is considered a timely death.

What stands out in this brief overview is that one's exact age at death is never known beforehand. And this is part of the gift of life and the gift of death. If individuals knew the day they were destined to die, this knowledge would eliminate the meaning with which death endows life. It is both the known and the unknown which together endow life with the search for meaning. It is the known aspect that death is the common denominator for all of humankind, and it is the unknown of the exact time of death that allows death to endow life with meaning.

If one's time of death were known, one would most probably not be able to utilize that information in a constructive manner. Illustrative is the case of a physician who informs a terminally ill cancer patient that he has three months or some other specific time to live. It is at that moment that the will to live, the desire to live a meaningful life, the hope to struggle in this world is usually significantly diminished. One does not have the capacity to live knowing the time of one's death. Yet, one only has the capacity to live knowing that one will eventually die. It is this paradox that is crucial in a new understanding of the phrase "premature death."

The phrase "premature death," understood literally, implies that death should come at a specific time. What is that specific time that is not considered premature? Is it when a person has grandchildren or great grandchildren? Is it when one has written one or two books? Is it when one has seen the beauty of Yosemite National Park or the Swiss Alps? Is it when one's children or grandchildren are married? "Premature death" is a phrase that usually brings untold grief to the mourners.

"Premature death" does, however, have meaning sociologically and psychologically. Man is not an island. As Aristotle stated, man is a social animal. I would modify Aristotle's statement to read: man is a social human being. In any case, man is social. Thus, in the case of a young mother dying, leaving behind small children, her death is premature. The small children still being dependent on maternal support are obviously affected by the death of the mother. In that sense, death is premature.

125

When a person dies one week before reaching his or her seventieth birthday, that is similar to the concept of a premature death. Frequently, the surviving spouse focuses primarily on and laments over that one week which the deceased failed to survive. Does that mean that dying on one's seventieth birthday is a more meaningful death? Is that a "good death" and death at sixty-nine years and fifty-one weeks is not a good death? It is the unknown time of everyone's death that instills meaning to one's entire life. As the violinist Nathan Milstein said, "I am glad I do not know when I am going to die. If I knew I could no longer enjoy myself" (Goodman, 1981, p. 39).

Man is the Image of God

Death comes at an unknown time to all individuals. Death is a natural outcome of life and is even considered as part of the scheme of creation of "very good." Yet, returning to our central question, why does the Torah also ascribe a punitive element to the natural process of dying?

God said to Adam that "On the day you eat from the Tree of Knowledge of Good and Evil you shall surely die" (Genesis 2:17). This certainly does not mean that Adam was created as an immortal and only by violating God's commandment did he become mortal. His violation did not bring death into the world. We have already demonstrated that life and aging and illness and death are all part of life, which is God-given. It also does not mean that on the day that Adam violated God's commandment he would die. He did not die. What does it mean?

Let us focus our attention on the fact that God commanded Adam. What does it mean that God spoke to man? What does it mean that God created a world where some things are beneficial for man and some things may not be beneficial? What does it mean that man was given free choice to either listen to God or disobey God's commandment? The fact that God talked to man and commanded man to act in a certain way teaches us two important concepts.

God considers man as a being with whom it is worthwhile to engage in a dialogue. Despite the fact that God is God and man is man, and the difference between God and man is metaqualitative, nevertheless there is a connecting link between God and man and that is an image, a shadow of God. The Torah states: "And God created man in His Image, in the Image of God He created him... "(Genesis 1:27). The word "image" in Hebrew (tzelem) is derived from the root of tzel meaning shade or shadow. This shade of God is the connecting link to man. This shade represents God's protective wings over His creatures. This thought is expressed in the daily evening service:

126

"Shelter us in the shadow of your wings; for You are our protecting and saving God" (Birnbaum, 1949, 261-262). The aspect that man's image shares with God is irrelevant, and the Torah does not share it with us. Jewish medieval Biblical commentators and philosophers advanced hypotheses on the nature of God's image which was given to man. The significance, however, is that man has a link to God which God has implanted in man forever.

Man is created in the Image of God. God is not an exemplary image of man; man is created in the Image of God. That is why what man thinks of God is so significant, because man is created in that Image. Abraham Joshua Heschel states:

> It is only in the light of what the biblical man thinks of God, namely a Being who created heaven and earth, the God of absolute justice and compassion, the master of nature and history who transcends nature and history, that the idea of man having been created in the image of God refers to the supreme mystery of man, of his nature and existence. (Heschel, 1972, p. 151)

We are told in the Torah that God is not man and man is not God (Numbers 23:19), and Isaiah states: "To Whom will you liken God? Or what likeness will you compare to Him?" (Isaiah 40:18). Nevertheless, man is created in the Image of God. This image may conceal more than it actually reveals. Whatever it connotes, it is this image of man that creates the special covenantal relationship between God and man.

Man is man because of his unique composite of earth and spirit (soul). This soul represents the Image of God. This image is not in man. It does not refer to a specific quality such as speech, reason, or skill. The image is man himself. It does not matter if this image is of Moses, Rembrandt, Einstein, or someone completely anonymous. This image does not depend on any achievement, virtue, or special talent. It is this special element which man possesses that creates the special God-man or man-God relationship.

Parenthetically, at the time of death of righteous individuals, the Image of God is removed from man by a kiss from God (Talmud, Moed Katan 28a). A kiss is a sign of love. Also, the kiss of death is God's sign of love for man. A kiss of death not only refers to a death not accompanied by agony, pain, and suffering - but spiritually it may also refer to the antithetical process of "and he breathed in his nostrils the breath of life and man became a living being" (Genesis 2:7). Man became a human being via "God's breath" and man's soul returns to God via "kiss inhaling." The Torah describes the death of Aaron and Moses via the mouth of God (Numbers 33:38; Deuteronomy

127

34:5). The Midrash comments: "When God retrieves the souls of righteous people, it is performed with a calm spirit" (Sifre, Deuteronomy 34:5). The Talmud conceptualizes this expression as referring to a kiss of death by God Himself (Moed Katan 28a). God embraces man and man's soul returns to the Creator.

The second principle which is derived from God's speaking to man and commanding him is the philosophical principle that man is given free will by being created as he was to either listen to the voice of God or ignore it. The Torah states: "Observe and hear all these words that I command you that it may go well with you and with your children after you forever, when you do that which is good and right in the eyes of the Lord your God" (Deuteronomy 12:28).

The Divine commandments, whether understood or not, are for the benefit of man (Deuteronomy 7:24). But, nevertheless, man has been given free will to either obey God's instructions or not.

This is the meaning of the mention of death which is associated with God's command of not eating from the Tree of Knowledge of Good and Evil. Man is responsible for his actions; he has been given free will and ultimately this free will is rescinded when death comes. God has brought death into the world as a natural part of life; God has even declared that death is "very good." Death has allowed man to have free will to either follow God's commandments or not - knowing that one day when spirit and flesh are no longer together, neither will there be the opportunity to serve God through our free will.

Life is the time allotted to serve God through free will. Judaism has always emphasized the here-and-now which exists prior to death, rather than the existence of the unknown after death. The Mishnah states: "Rabbi Jacob said: one hour spent in repentance and good deeds in this world is better than the whole life of the world to come..." (Abot 4:17). Repentance and good deeds are dependent on man's free will to serve God. This ability is non-existent in the world to come.

Life, Death and Eternal Life

Is there a world to come and what do we know about it based on the Torah? What do we know based on empirical reality? Spirit and flesh cannot coexist forever and therefore, death is a natural process. What happens to flesh and what happens to the spirit? Flesh decomposes entirely and returns to its natural elements of earth. The Torah states: "...until you return to the land, for out of it you were taken, for you are earth and to earth shall you return" (Genesis 3:19). And King

128

Solomon states: "...everything came from dust and everything returns to dust" (Ecclesiastes 3:20).

Although the Torah tells us that flesh decomposes completely, we are not told in the Torah what happens to the spirit. The Torah states: "And the Lord God formed the man of earth from the land and breathed into his nostrils the breath of life and man became a living being" (Genesis 2:17). Initially, man was composed of earth, and the breath of life (the same word as soul) was instilled in man and he became a living being. Nowhere in the Torah are we told what happens to the soul when man dies. King Solomon states that the soul returns to its Creator (Ecclesiastes 12:7). G.F. Moore (1969) and E.E. Urbach (1969) devote a large part of their work in Jewish theology to trying to understand the soul, the Messianic era, the hereafter, eschatology, and many related concepts. The common denominator of these concepts is that there is some form of soul-life after death. Their theology is based primarily on Rabbinic literature. Similarly, medieval Jewish philosophers devote major parts of their works to these issues. All the statements are mere speculation but one thing is clear - some form of existence of the eternal soul is axiomatic.

The psycho-Halakhic man of conscience is derived from the fact that the very special gift of "death" drives man to understand God's demands objectively, experience Divinity subjectively, and utilize his conscience to equilibrate the subject/object dichotomy. The reality of the finiteness of this life creates the realization that the significance of the present moment encourages the psycho-Halakhic man of conscience to ultimately rely on his understanding of the Divine word.

When our forefathers Abraham and Isaac die, each is gathered to his people (Genesis 25:8, 35:29). This expression suggests an important concept. Frequently the dying patient experiences existential loneliness. He justifiably feels that no one else is facing the same unknown as he is. He may be surrounded by family and friends and yet feel lonely. Just as man enters this world singularly and alone, he exits this world in a unique existential situation of the human predicament - loneliness. The Torah, however, well aware of this aspect of man's singularity, informs man that after death he is gathered to his people - his earthly departure represents only temporal loneliness; his celestial community is permanent. Thus, the afterlife is symbolically represented as a community of souls.

The belief in the eternity of the soul is seemingly derived from the fact that man is created in God's Image. The Bible notes that man is formed from the earth to which he ultimately returns when he dies (Ecclesiastes 12:7), and the Image of God - that which emanated from God's breath - returns to God Who

129

gave it (Ecclesiastes 12:7). Thus, death represents two distinct and dichotomous experiences. On the one hand, death represents a return to earth, a complete decomposition of the form of man. On the other hand, death is the leap into eternity. From this perspective, death also represents a reunion of man's Divine Image, his soul, to the ultimate source of Being - Divinity itself. The form of that existence after death remains an unfathomable mystery. The link, however, is a relatedness to God - the source of our life. Despite this relatedness of the soul of man to God, Judaism has always emphasized the quality of being in this earthly world, where man has been given the opportunity to freely serve God or not to do so.

The Torah rarely deals with death as a problem. The Torah does mention that when great people (e.g., Jacob, Aaron, Moses - people who served as teachers and leaders to the rest of their people) died, the Israelites mourned for thirty days (Genesis 50:10; Numbers 20:20; Deuteronomy 34:8). During this period of mourning, some of the teachings of Moses were forgotten (Talmud, Moed Katan 30a). The Torah also states: "...and the days of weeping and mourning for Moses were ended" (Deuteronomy 34:8). The emphasis in reacting to the death of Moses was not a degradation of life - but, on the contrary, the emphasis was on the termination of mourning and the return to an emphasis on life.

The Talmud states: "Rabbi Judah said in the name of Samuel: Three thousand laws were forgotten during the mourning period after Moses's death" (Temurah 16a). The sadness over Moses's death is reflected in the lack of leadership for the living people. The people are bereft of a leader.
Similarly, the Talmud relates:

> Any rending of clothes not done at the time of death is not a proper rending...when they told Rabbi Johanan, 'The soul of Rabbi Hanina has gone to rest; he rent on account of him thirteen robes of wool and said: 'Gone is the man before whom I trembled!'
>
> Rabbis are in a different category, since their discussions are always recalled - it is for us like the time of death. (Moed Katan 24a)

The death of a rabbi is emotionally and intellectually felt whenever his teachings are missed. Again, the emphasis is that the living people miss their leader.

Life is the one opportunity to serve God voluntarily before the ultimate and eternal leap, where the freedom to choose to serve God no longer exists.

130

Jewish pietists have never longed for the eternal life after death. The psycho-_Halakhic_ man of conscience also seeks to pursue "eternity" in the here-and-now. He seeks the ultimate of each moment for its sacred uniqueness. He is able to sanctify the moment into an everlasting moment.

Thus, death is a transition from previously potential eternity to actual eternity. Time after death is eternal; time prior to death can become eternal via sanctifying the present moment by living with meaning. But ultimately, the life-after becomes a matter of faith. The anxiety regarding death represents the anxiety of the unknown after death. In the core of our soul, we hope that the great mystery of being will receive some clarification in the hereafter. The pain and suffering of mankind call out for a solution to the enigma of life on earth.

Halakhic reality also recognizes the "potential eternity" of the here-and-now. This means that man's behavior remains in the unwritten annals of mankind's history. Maimonides states:

> ...sins which were confessed on this DAY of Atonement one confesses again on subsequent DAYS of Atonement although he has not subsequently transgressed them. As it is stated:
> "My transgression I know and my sin is constant."
> (Mishneh Torah, Teshubah 2:8)

This statement, although referring to a sin, applies to good deeds as well. Man's past behavior exists forever - in his history as well as the history of mankind. Even when a person has died - his deeds, good or bad, have achieved eternity.

Van den Berg explains man's relationship to time by theorizing that future and past are embodied in the present. He states: "The past is within the present: What was is the way it is appearing now. The future: what comes, the way it is meeting us now" (Van den Berg, 1972, p. 91). The present contains the selected perceptions of the past and the anticipated visions of the future. The flickering momentary effervescent present is synonymous with the past, present, and future. This merging of three different time dimensions applies to the individual and to the collective - in the here-and-now and the eternal future.

The concept of _Zekhut Abot_ (the merit of our fathers) can be understood as reflecting upon the deceased's eternal good deeds. The Mishnah states: "...and all who work with the community, let them work with sincere devotion, for the merit of the community's fathers sustains the communal workers, and

131

the righteousness of the fathers endures forever" (Abot 2:2). When leaders of a community engage in difficult endeavors on behalf of the community and succeed, the leaders should realize that their ultimate success is related to the merit of the ancestry of the communal works. The fathers' merits are regarded as eternal.

This concept of Zekhut Abot can be explained psychologically as well as theologically. Both explanations are not only not mutually exclusive, but indeed complementary. Psychologically, a positive image of one's parents and ancestors can serve as a positive modeling force in a person's life. This principle is demonstrated as the motivating factor in Joseph's refraining from having sexual relations with Potiphar's wife. The Talmud says: "At that moment his father's image came and appeared to him through the window..." (Sotah 36b). Theologically, the meritorious deeds and image of one's father are in existence eternally. They serve as a "protective" shadow over the future generations. In God's perception, the span of a thousand years is like yesterday. As the Psalmist says: "Indeed, a thousand years in your sight are like a day that passes, like a watch in the night" (Psalms 90:4).

Thus, even when one's existence after death is exclusively in the soul dimension, one's temporal life coexists eternally with the new eternity of after-life. Zekhut Abot, the merits of one's parents' behavior, that which is achieved in one's earthly domain, continue on in one's after-life, protecting one's future generations in this earthly domain. The inevitableness of death and its naturalness as part of the very fabric of the creation of man are described very poignantly by Rabbi Eliezer Hakapar who states: "Everyone who is born is destined to die...Against your will you were created, Against your will you were born, Against your will you will die" (Mishnah, Abot 4:22). Death is a natural part of life. Another indication of the naturalness of death is manifested by the blessing which is recited by people who are present at the time of death, or by mourners at the time of the funeral. The Talmud cites the blessing as: "Blessed be He who is a true Judge" (Berakhot 59b). By reciting this blessing we acknowledge that God, who is the source of all blessings, is also the source of death, which is considered a blessing for the individual. In God's infinite wisdom (and a Judge represents the epitome of wisdom and justice), death is a blessing, just as life is a blessing.

The Lonely Journey

What are some of the psychological and sociological implications of our theological thoughts. Initially, the aloneness of dying seems to imply an overwhelmingly frightening experience. The awareness of approaching death should actually

132

accentuate the need to live authentically.

Throughout life, attempts are constantly being made to mitigate the loneliness of life. Life is shared through relationships with parents, children, a spouse or other relatives and friends. Existentially, however, the more that life is shared together, the more one often feels one's own individuality and loneliness. During beautiful and intimate moments of mutual togetherness, one's distinctiveness and separateness surfaces. This dialectic pendulum of momentary self-oblivion only serves to emphasize the sense of utter aloneness which follows. Similarly, immersion into work, projects, goals and activities focuses our thoughts beyond ourselves. This outer directedness is transient, however prolonged its duration. Sometimes, in the midst or after involvement in work, the self emerges, recognizing the distinctiveness of "self" from the previous obliviousness of self.

Throughout life, the aloneness of life is mitigated, denied, and attenuated via outer directedness, either sharing with people or immersion into work. In contrast, however, is the aloneness of facing death. Despite the fact that death is universal, experiencing death is an event that is by its very nature non-communicative and individualistic, and it therefore remains a mystery.

Furthermore, the person facing death feels utterly alone in this journey. Sometimes, he may imagine meeting God or a deceased parent, but he is always alone on this journey. The dying patient is partially comforted by empathic caring and love - but he travels alone.

Death Confers Meaning on Life

The most common emotion of dying patients is their anxiety and fear of death. Patients are aware that this road is traveled alone. All facades and pretentiousness are usually disclaimed for integrity and authenticity. The patient laments all of his unfinished tasks, the superficial relationships, and the transitoriness of life. These reflections are equally applicable to a healthy individual. Death, however, does not come only at the end of one's lifetime. Each moment of our life is a dying moment which disappears into no-thing or nothingness. Every second of our lives disappears and never returns. Not only is all of life temporary and finite, but also every day, every hour, and every minute has that same characteristic.

Death and the dying of every moment create life. If life were infinite, there would be no death, no aging, no illness and no need to do anything now! Everything could be postponed.

133

One could wait a week, a year, or an infinite time because nothing would have to be done immediately. There would be no situation or opportunity that would require immediate action, because everything could be delayed ad infinitum.

We are called upon to act immediately because of the pressure of the finitude of existence, the urgency of time passing, and the opportunities passing before our eyes. Each moment of life is endowed with potential meaningfulness. Only unfulfilled potentialities are dying; only unactualized acts are transitory. Once a good deed or negative act is actualized, it is deposited into the everlasting past from where nothing and nobody can remove it. This eternal time capsule contains all of our experience, including not only our deeds, but also how we face illness, aging, suffering, and even death. Towards the end of the prayers on Yom Kippur we recite: "O Thou, Who hears the voice of weeping, may it be Your will to conserve our tears...for we hopefully look to you alone" (Birnbaum, 1951, p. 1000). God collects and treasures our tears in a vessel. The human capacity to cope with life's difficulties is part of God's eternal treasure (Frankl, 1983).

All of life is deposited in an eternal time capsule. Instead of focusing on life's transitoriness and finiteness, emphasis is placed on actualized moments, the fulfilled potentials, and even on the attitude and coping capacity vis-a-vis pain and suffering. Human dignity does not depend on any "usefulness" or social value. Real dignity reflects the values with which people have lived their lives. This dignity can never be deleted. It is inscribed in the history of the world and in the lives of our children and grandchildren.

Death confers meaning on life. Death is not primarily a scientific biological phenomenon, when the heart and lungs cease to function. Death and dying are a life-long process that create the will to live. Death is the best friend to life. Death allows life to be lived to its fullest potential. Not only is death the final stage of growth (Kubler-Ross, 1975), it is the life-long catalyst to live a meaningful life.

Fear of death is primarily fear of dying prematurely, before one has actualized one's potential or before one has achieved self-actualization. People fear that they may die when their life is still incomplete. This potential incompleteness represents the existential fear of death. If this state of incompleteness comes prior to one's death, the patient has a very difficult time coming to terms with death. Butler (1963) showed that old or terminally ill patients accept death much more easily when such patients do not feel that their life has been incomplete. The ultimate existential crisis is the everyday crisis of a normal day and how to live that day.

Feifel (1965) states that the primary human crisis in facing death is reflecting upon talents and opportunities which have not been implemented.

This concept of prematurity and incompleteness refers not only to a specific self-actualization or self-fulfillment, but also to authentic living in the present. What behaviors are appropriate and what behaviors are inappropriate in the here-and-now? Living authentically refers to the unspoken words we wanted to say but did not say and which must forever remain unsaid. Living meaningfully refers also to regrets about thoughts and feelings never shared.

Only when death is an intimate part of our life do we live and die without regrets. Every moment in life can become as important as the last moment of our life.The Biblical and Halakhic man of conscience strives for that goal.

References

Birnbaum, P. (1949). Daily Prayer Book. New York: Hebrew Publishing Company.

Birnbaum, P. (1951). High Holyday Prayer Book. New York: Hebrew Publishing Company.

Butler, R.N. (1963). "The Life Review: An Interpretation of Reminiscence in the Aged," Psychiatry, 119, 721-728.

Feifel, H. (1965). "The Functions of Attitudes Towards Death," Death and Dying: Attitudes of Patient and Doctor. 5, 632-641.

Frankl, V.E. (1983). The Meaning of Suffering. Videocassette. Health Science Information Center. Los Angeles: Cedars-Sinai Medical Center.

Goodman, L.M. (1981). Death and the Creative Life. New York: Springer Publishing Company.

Heschel, A.J. (1972). The Insecurity of Freedom. New York: Schocken Books.

The Holy Scriptures (1985). Philadelphia: Jewish Publication Society.

Kasher, M. (Ed.) (1944). Biblical Encyclopedia. Volume 2. New York: American Biblical Encyclopedia Society.

Kubler-Ross, E. (1975). Death: The Final Stage of Growth. Prentice-Hall: Englewood Cliffs, New Jersey.

Maimonides, M. (12th Century) (1962). Mishneh Torah (6 Vols.). New York: M.P. Press.

Meier, L. (1986). "The Psycho-Halakhic Man of Conscience," Journal of Psychology and Judaism, 10 (2), 19-45.

Midrash (10 Vols.). (1961). H. Freedman and M. Simons (Eds.). London: Soncino Press.

Moore, G.F. (1969). Judaism. Cambridge: Harvard University Press.

Sifre. In Malbim, M. (19th Century) (1964). Commentary to the Pentateuch: Deuteronomy. New York: Grossman.

Talmud (18 Vols.). (1961). I. Epstein (Ed.). London: Soncino Press.

Urbach, E.E. (1969). The Sages: Their Concepts and Beliefs (Hebrew). Jerusalem: Magnes Press, The Hebrew University.

Van den Berg, J.H. (1972). A Different Existence. Pittsburgh: Duquesne University Press.

Zohar (5 Vols.). (1984). London: Soncino Press.

CHAPTER 9

Epilogue

Introduction

In my earlier chapter (2), entitled <u>Reflections on a Spiritual Dream</u>, Erwin Altman was represented as Mr. Solomon. He signified the stage which exists <u>beyond</u> the conflict of psychology and religion. He emanated the refreshing spirit of ongoing, dynamic inner growth, during which the inner dialectic with doubt is a stimulating friend towards integration of faith and doubt. As he ascended Jacob's Ladder of Ascension, he demonstrated how faith and doubt can coexist in a harmonious way. I hope that the reader will find his words and thoughts eternally inspirational. This is why the author feels privileged to be able to include this epilogue in this volume.

Biographical Note
on
Erwin Altman, J.D.

ERWIN ALTMAN, the second son of Chief Rabbi Dr. Adolf (Abraham) Altmann and his wife Malwine, nee Weisz, was born on the 20th of January 1908 in Salzburg, Austria. His father was then Rabbi of the Jewish Community in Salzburg, thereafter Senior Chaplain of the Austrian - Hungarian Army. After the First World War he became the Chief Rabbi of Trier, the oldest Jewish Community in Germany. Erwin's happy childhood and youth was shared with his elder brother Alexander, his younger sister, Hilda, and his younger brothers, Manfred and Wilhelm.

Their father, an early pioneer of religious Zionism, an illustrious Rabbi, historian and philosopher, and their mother, the guardian angel of her family and her community, imbued them with their great Rabbinic, scholarly and cultural family tradition.

Erwin devoted the first period of his academic studies to comprehensive Jewish studies at the world famous Hildesheimer Rabbinical Seminary in Berlin. These were followed by his years of university studies of law, leading to his Doctorate of Jurisprudence with highest distinction, at the end of 1933; he was one of the last Jews to achieve this degree under the Nazi rule.

The Nazi era led to his emigration in 1934 to Holland, where his sister Hilda was married and living with her family. He became legal adviser to a Dutch company. His brother Manfred, who had completed his university law studies with Erwin, also emigrated to Holland as legal adviser to another company, and their brother Wilhelm came to Holland as a student of chemistry. Their oldest brother, Alexander, remained in Berlin as Rabbi of the Jewish community and Professor at the Rabbinical Seminary. Their parents stayed in Trier, as they did not wish to leave their community.

Only as late as 1938 did the parents leave Trier and settle in The Hague, Holland. In that same year, Alexander received a call from the Jewish Community in Manchester, England, to become their leading, "Communal Rabbi." In 1939, Manfred was able to settle in London as adviser on international law to a London company.

When war broke out in 1939, all efforts for the emigration of the other members of the family failed. Erwin decided to risk the mine fields in the Atlantic Ocean and journey by ship to North America in order to try to arrange permission for them to come to America.

In spite of his and his brothers' tremendous efforts, this could not be achieved. When Holland was invaded, Erwin was in the United States and was thus saved, but his parents, sister and her family and his youngest brother Wilhelm were all deported, victims of the Holocaust in Auschwitz, sharing this fate with millions of other Jews.

After a period of great difficulties in the U.S.A., Erwin decided to embark on a new career, in the Civil Service within the Department of Public Social Services of Los Angeles County, California. There, in a long and distinguished career leading to a directorial capacity, he did specialized pioneering work in selfless dedication to the social and spiritual rehabilita-

141

tion and rescue of countless fellowmen.

After his retirement, he continued with great intensity his research and wide interests in Jewish and general cultural matters.

The impact of his personality is reflected in the published brochure entitled MORENU, Our REVERED TEACHER, GUIDE AND COUNSELOR, a Singular Award Ceremony and Tribute to an Outstanding Personality, ERWIN ALTMAN, J.D., edited by Rabbi Levi Meier, Ph.D., Chaplain, Cedars-Sinai Medical Center (1986).

It is the record of a special ceremony, unique in the setting of the Cedars-Sinai Medical Center, when the award of the distinguished Hebrew title Morenu - our revered Teacher, Guide and Counselor was bestowed on Erwin Altman, and a special diploma was presented to him on December 27, 1985. The preface to this brochure is reproduced on the following page.

Erwin died on May 6, 1986 and was survived by two distinguished brothers: his older brother Alexander, Emeritus Professor of Jewish Philosophy and History of Ideas at Brandeis University, and Associate of Harvard University; and by his younger brother, Manfred, of London, England, a Governor of the Institute of Jewish Studies, University College, London, England. The family suffered a further loss when, on June 6, 1987, Professor Alexander Altmann passed away.

During Erwin's prolonged illness, he continued to record his reflections on life and death. It has been my distinct honor and privilege to serve as his Rabbi while he was a patient in Cedars-Sinai Medical Center. The preface of the Morenu (1986) document is also reprinted here as a living testimony to his outstanding spiritual personality and his lifelong devotion to his life motto, "Be a Blessing."

The second Annual Psychology and Judaism Conference, held in Los Angeles, California, on February 8, 1987, was dedicated to his memory; and excerpts from his "Reflections on this Thing and No-Thing called Life and Death" edited by me were read at the Conference.

This is the text of the preface of the <u>Morenu</u> brochure, mentioned in the biographical note.

In the midst of the preparation of this Tribute brochure, the esteemed recipient of the <u>Morenu</u> (Our Revered Teacher) Award, Erwin Altman, J.D. - who was looking forward to seeing the printed brochure - received the kiss of God and was called to his Eternal Life on May 6, 1986. That this day, the 27th of Nissan, 5746, was <u>Yom Hashoah</u>, Holocaust Remembrance Day, was no coincidence.

Most of his family shared the fate of the millions who were martyred victims of the Holocaust, and his own life was deeply disrupted by it. He was "gathered to his people" (in the Biblical language of Genesis 25:8) on this sacred day of our people. We can only meditate on the symbolic and spiritual dimensions of this awe-inspiring synchronicity.

The title <u>Morenu</u> has an honored tradition in Jewish history. It was, since the 14th century, associated with specific academic achievements; later - including our century - it reflected rabbinic or semi-rabbinic qualifications and also served as a title of distinction for outstanding spiritual status in the Jewish community.

In our ceremony, the title <u>Morenu</u> is, with utmost modesty and humility, being bestowed on Erwin Altman, J.D., in recognition of his universal studies and his wisdom; his outstanding spiritual personality; his lifelong devotion to his life motto, "Be a Blessing;" and his exceptional qualities and achievements, as expressed in the citation of the <u>Morenu</u> diploma presented to him.

The impact of the <u>Morenu</u> ceremony is multidimensional. That this exceptional ceremony, recognizing his inspirational impact on all of us, took place during his stay as a patient in the Hospice Unit of Cedars-Sinai Medical Center, made it an historic occasion. The ceremony itself became a source of inspiration not only for the recipient, but also for all of us who participated in it. The spiritual message of his philosophy of life, and the thoughts expressed during the ceremony remain timeless and meaningful, much like an "Ethical Will."

The historic implications of bestowing the title <u>Morenu</u> under these unique circumstances will affect and intensify future chaplain-patient relationships. It is clear that an important link in these relationships is the spirituality emanating from the patient's specific spiritual merits and resourcefulness.

143

Mr. Altmann was a shining example for us. With his deep, uplifting philosophy and love of life, he maintained his hope throughout and supported it by his indomitable will and spirit. He chose to retain his conscious, creative mental and spiritual faculties rather than let the great agonies of pain and suffering of cancer control the quality of his life. He was able to transform this reality to a higher spiritual dimension by his messianic outlook and faith in Eternal Life. Even during the very last phase of his life, God granted him his wish; he rallied and, fully himself, was clearly communicating messages of love and prayer.

Initially, this brochure was to be presented in the spirit of L'Hayyim, "To Life," representing Mr. Erwin Altman's consistent living a life of blessings. Now, this brochure has an added dimension: Yizkor -- "In Memoriam."

However, even "In Memoriam," this perpetuates Erwin Altman's life motto "Be a Blessing," as his memory will continue to be a blessing for us and for Eternal Life.

Excerpts From
"Reflections
On This Thing and No-Thing
Called Life and Death"

BY
ERWIN ALTMAN, J.D.

Edited by

Rabbi Levi Meier, Ph.D.

About the Abrahamic Divine Calling Veheyeh Berakhah,
"And be a Blessing," and its Interrelationship with
Zekher Tzaddik Livrakhah - "May the Memory of the
Righteous be a Blessing."

The first relates to life, the second to death. But is
this so? I feel there is a deep interrelationship which links
both together.

A central theme throughout the history of philosophy,
religion, and psychology is the discussion of the concept of an
inner imperative which urges man to find meaning and direction
in life.

The dramatic Biblical report on Abraham's earthly
pilgrimage - governed by God's commands - mirrors his spiritual
pilgrimage following his inner commands in a dynamic dialogue
within himself. Abraham's awakening, from the darkness of idol
worship to his faith in one unified and unifying eternal God,
leads to his inner revelation and to the Divine response giving
meaning and direction in life for him and his future generations in just two words, Veheyeh Berakhah - "And Be a Blessing"
(Genesis 12:2).

The basis of God's responsive call is His love for all His
creations; the stage of inner development and consciousness
allows those who are ready for sacrifices to become His torch
bearers and to understand the full potential of man's destiny.
(A typical example of God's affirmations of His love is in
Deuteronomy 7:6-8.)

Man's destiny to "Be A Blessing" can be conceived on
various levels. It proclaims the constructive principle
against any destructive tendencies. It means love in thought,
words and action. But it has deeper dimensions. Veheyeh ("and
be") has the same four Hebrew letters as Adonay, the "Name" of
God, revealed to Moses (Exodus 3:4) and used in Verse 1 of
Genesis 12 in speaking to Abraham. The unfathomable meaning of
this "Name" is the concept of God proclaiming "I AM THAT I WAS,
I AM THAT I AM, I AM THAT I SHALL BE," the "ETERNAL PRESENCE."

The position of the letters Vav and Yud is different within
the word Veheyeh, but it is composed of the same four Hebrew
letters as the Name of God. This allows us to suggest a deeply
meaningful interpretation.

"And Be a Blessing" - Veheyeh Berakhah addresses man's
higher self, saying: by your faith and fulfillment of God's
call, "Be a Blessing," you reach a stage of understanding of
its highest spiritual meaning: Veheyeh - you are that you were,
you are that you are, you are that you shall be --- a
146

continuous potential source of blessing, as you are an eternal 'partner' within God's love and His eternity.

This is addressed not to mankind in general collective terms, but to Abraham and to each individual in each generation, as each is created in the Image of God, which is a basic Biblical concept.

It leads to our faith in the eternal dimension within the "wholeness" of man, to the this-worldly and transworldly dimension of man's destiny to "Be A Blessing." But the emphasis is on man's actualization of his destiny within history, in the here-and-now, in the evolution of his consciousness (to enable him to grasp the potentialities of comprehending this cosmic universe) and of his responsibility: to use his comprehension to be and to become more and more "A Blessing," for the "wholeness" of himself and of all the creations of the universe. By accepting the pathways - the Torah, the guiding signposts of Jewish law and tradition - in his pilgrimage within and without, he experiences the inner dynamics of the challenge of the Divine call. By our faith in the eternal dimension of man, which we call soul, we gain the spiritual energies to respond to this call, and by making "Being A Blessing" the central reality of our life, we become "holy." The Divine call to be a "holy people" is identical with the Divine call to "Be A Blessing," if we experience both as linked with the eternal dimension of man.

Faith in the eternal dimension of the soul - the subject of a wide spectrum of varied opinions in the history of Jewish tradition, philosophy and mysticism - has, I feel, a deeply embedded place in the spiritual world of the Jewish people.

This eternity is reflected, for instance, in the words of Samuel (1,25:9), "The human soul will be bound in the bundle of living in the care of the Lord, our God." Or in Ecclesiastes (12:7), "The spirit of man returns to God, who gave it." The Talmud (Niddah 30b) speaks of the angel who puts his finger on the upper lip of each newly born child and says: "And now forget all and learn afresh." (The allegory adds that this is why we have a little groove in the center of the upper lip!)

In the light of our interpretations of the Divine call Veheyeh Berakhah, "And Be a Blessing," the sacred Jewish custom to add to the name of a departed righteous person the words Zekher Tzaddik Livrakhah - "May the memory of the righteous be a blessing" - assumes a spiritual meaning of complementing the Divine call "Be A Blessing."

This "blessedness" and "blessingness" of a tzaddik's (a righteous person's) living memory is - I feel - nothing else

147

but a _continuation_ of his life - and after-life - program to fulfill the Divine calling, "Be A Blessing," eternally.

The concept of _Berakhah_, "Blessing," now becomes a bridge between our dimension and eternity.

These three words for the departed -- _Zekher Tzaddik Livrakhah_ -- are prayers containing deep layers of meaning for the relationship between living man, God and the departed.

The conscious remembrance combined with blessing is a spiritual act - a spiritual _experience_ of the impact of the departed's soul on our conscious, subconscious and unconscious.

It means a prayer for mutual blessings between us and the departed's soul, between us and God, between God and the departed: We pray that:

> the _departed_ may be blessed by God in his ascent, in dimensions unfathomable to us, to continue his spiritual destiny of "Be A Blessing" within God's love and eternity,

> that _we_ may be blessed by the ongoing inspiration emanating from his soul's impact on us, from our memory of the past and from keeping _our_ memory tuned in to our faith in his eternity in God's eternal love, and

> that _we_ bless God for allowing us the spiritual experience of this continuing impact as a reminder of our _own_ eternal destiny to "Be a Blessing," making _Him_ and _us_ continuing partners in fulfilling our eternal destinies.

What is meant by this all-important word, _Berakhah_, "Blessing"? The Midrash (Genesis 12:2) reminds us that the change of one vowel transforms the meaning into "spring of water" (_Berekhah_). In our context we may say that man's existential presence in our dimension is transformed by "Being a Blessing" into a dynamic "spring of water," a vitalizing, purifying source of thoughts, words and actions, allowing the flow of Divine energies to inspire the higher self in man and the whole universe to become whole and transparent, and so become holy as God's partner in eternity and love.

Tolstoy was inspired to say: The Jew is that sacred being, who has brought down from heaven the everlasting fire, and has illumined with it the entire world. He is the religious source, spring and fountain, out of which all the rest of the peoples have drawn their beliefs and their religions. (quoted

148

in Hertz, 1943, p. 4)

This Divine fire, the core of Judaism, is first and most meaningfully expressed in the Abrahamic calling, Veheyeh Berakhah - "And Be a Blessing." It is echoed - as I tried to show - with the same meaning in Zekher Tzaddik Livrakhah, - "May the memory of the righteous be a blessing;" both are focused on our life and beyond our life, unifying both dimensions within the continuum of God's love and eternity.

A Meditative Reflection on the Meaning of the Words, "My Life," "My Death," and "After-Life"

It is encouraging that there are signs in our time that religious meditation is taken more seriously in scientific circles and psychological research and practice. Einstein's words, "The cosmic religious experience is the strongest and noblest driving force behind scientific research, "(1985, p. 39) are finding more echo in our time than in his. There is even some talk of scientists seeking "a sanctuary from materialistic science." I feel that the shadows of intellectual doubt encourage rather than hinder spiritual search and they each help "to clear the path." The dimension of religious faith is more and more recognized as belonging to a different plateau in the human psyche and does not hinder us from trying to reach the limits of the ever-expanding horizon of human understanding and research.

Within the limited time and capacity of our physical life span we can only use a language which draws its symbols and range of meaning from the evolution of our experiences. In religious meditation we allow ourselves to question the ultimate truth of "experiences," and we try to have glimpses of the truth by the notions of the "inconceivable, unlimited meta-reality" beyond the concepts of division between subject and object, experiencer and experience. It could be an "Ultimate - True - Reality" not of "Nothingness," but of "NO-THING-NESS," perhaps in the direction of the Jewish mystical concepts of Ayin in its manifold layers of meaning; in this context, consideration of the Eastern mystical concept of Nirvana is interesting.

These inner concepts are more than contemplation; they lead to the first steps on the "Ladder of Ascension" (Genesis 28:12), to become a life-transcendent, eternally fresh and refreshing fountain and resource, an instrument and vessel radiating blessings and grace elements, a transparent mirror of the Divine Image.

Perhaps even when the "I" of an individual passes away and the "thing-ly self" as an entity is dissolved, an "un-thing-

149

ly," "undifferentiated meta-whole," uncomposed of so-called "parts," could represent "my I-Identity," taking it over without a totally impersonal merger, thus "eternalizing" the purified true and unique personal spiritual worth and value by an inseparable bond of everlasting union. This could mean more than just a permanently kept-up memory-record, but also a time-lessly-affiliated, uniquely powerful and actively potent resource of special outgoing blessings. What is "earthly" of man will die, but his soul and its intrinsic core of essential goodness and merits, in Hebrew called Zekhuyot, will, as a collective cohesive unit, remain potently and meaningfully alive eternally. They are represented - symbolically - by the "angels" who on the two-way "Ladder of Ascension" go up from our dimension to the Divine and go down, on the other side of the two-way ladder, from the Divine to our dimension, in a continuous dynamic movement.

The unity of Zekhuyot (merits) and man's calling, Veheyeh Berakhah - "And Be a Blessing," is the pillar structure on which the eternal dynamic movement on the Ladder of Ascension and Descension depends, as a bridge of the emanation of God's love in all dimensions.

Man's aim in the here-and-now is centered in his realiza-tion that he is responsible for his part in this continuum, both as giver and recipient of love. This leads to walking in the Divine path in daily life; true self-realization by the love of one's self and of all fellowmen and all creations; inspirational and uplifting love and joy of life; honest search for truth in all spheres; the search for creative expansion of one's unique potentialities; the service of God through prayer and contemplation, and above all, through service to mankind and the universe by the spirituality of thought, word, and action.

On Symbols

In my spiritual search and inner experience, symbols play a great role. When the language of intellectual reason, of psychological concepts, becomes inadequate, when the metaphysi-cal, intuitive, religious experiences and vistas need a language, symbols assume the role of an illustrative, rich language.

Gershom Scholem says in his essay on the Magen David (Shield of David) in The Messianic Idea in Judaism and Other Essays on Jewish Spirituality:

When a man's world possesses spiritual meaning for him, when all his relations to the world around him
150

are conditioned by the living contents of this meaning, then and only then does this meaning crystallize and manifest itself in symbols. (1971, p. 257)

Something of the secret of man is poured into his symbols. The great symbols serve to express the unity of his world. If this be true for the individual, it is true to an even greater extent of the symbols which are adopted by a group, a community or a people...a lightning-like illumination. (1971, pp. 257-258)

I wish to add that such adoption by the individual or a people of a symbol is therefore not a deliberate, conscious act of selection, but occurs as an inner spark which illuminates the intuitive heritage with a spiritual charge, creating and responding to an inner revelation-type experience through the potency of the impact of the total structure, the "gestalt," of the symbol. I believe the imaginative, conscious and subconscious interplay between intellect and emotion creates a high degree of inner dynamic movement. This helps to unlock the depth of the intuitive faculty in man which needs and creates a multi-dimensional language of spiritual potency beyond conceptual, allegorical, visual and emotional communication levels.

As "symbol" comes from the Greek language and means "to bring together the parts," it is an inspired tool for our search for spirituality, in which all parts of conscious, subconscious and unconscious reality merge. The symbol itself becomes a rare and powerful resource for creativity and blissful union with the searching genius of a people.

My special interest in and love for the main symbols of the Jewish people, for their origins and links with universal and with specific Jewish resources, with Biblical, prophetical, historical and contemporary experiences, is responding to this impact.

A true symbol and its spiritual understanding can act like a magnetic needle moving under the surface of a field on which a random mass of iron particles assumes direction and order. Such magnetic power emanates from the mysterious quality of the impact of the intuitive message of the symbol and its spiritual charge. I feel it is also our task to discern where symbols are and can be used in the service of the opposing destructive powers and tendencies trying to undermine true spirituality. Our Abrahamic mission "Be a Blessing" warns us to be on our guard against these real dangers.

By making all dynamic aspects of the spiritual and opposing potencies of the various symbols conscious in us, we can turn them into blessings for modern man in search of dynamic har-

151

mony, in his inner and outer development.

About the "Light of Life"

Light is experienced by the human psyche as full consciousness leading to "enlightenment." It emerges from the dark
shadows of the subconscious and unconscious dimensions. We
acknowledge by our senses and by the experience of our scientific mind many phenomena relating to the broad concept of
"light." The colorful radiation of the human aura, the
emerging knowledge of "electric" energies, of "light" and
"energy" "frequencies" are beyond real comprehension, yet
govern the human body-mind system and the functioning of the
universe. As our horizon of knowledge and awareness is constantly expanding, our intuition grows but new mysteries
emerge.

Old mystical concepts and symbols receive illuminating old
and new meanings through modern insights, but these continue to
point even more to an unfathomable "beyond" behind the expanded
horizon of comprehension and experience.

The Jewish concept of Ner Tamid, the "Eternal Light," is
symbolic of our faith in the presence, within our inner and
outer dimension, of the reflection of the Shekhinah, of the
"Divine Presence of God," which sustains man and the universe,
"here and now" and "there and then" and in dimensions "beyond"
our space-time concepts.

The centrality of this "light" principle both as psychic
fact and as a description of one of nature's phenomena is highlighted through symbols. We find such symbols relating to
"light" in all cultures and esoteric traditions. The main
Jewish symbol in this context is the Menorah (candelabrum),
shaped like a tree and representing with its base, stem and
seven branches the "tree of life." The seven branches are lit
by the holy fire, by the light emanating from the Ten Commandments which were carried, accompanied by the Menorah, throughout the pilgrimage of the Jewish people in the wilderness and
throughout history. The Menorah became the Jewish people's
"portable" tree of life, inspiring it to become itself a
burning Menorah, a light to itself and "a light to the nations"
(Isaiah 42:6), carrying the torch of man's enlightenment by his
acceptance of being the Image of his Divine source of
existence.

In the world of numerology, particularly in its specific
Jewish tradition, but also in scientific concepts, the numbers
7 and 10 have great significance in the functioning of the
universe. In oriental religious science, "life energy" is
mystically conceived as sustaining man through his inner system

of seven major Chakras, the vision of an ascending ladder-type structure leading from the lowest to the highest Chakra. In the great mystical tradition of Kabbalah, the "tree of man" and the "tree of life" are related to the seven (lower) Sefirot and the three higher, making a total of ten Sefirot. They reflect the inner path of man's soul guided by the Divine fires burning within him, emerging from Ain Sof and striving for the multidimensional, inseparable dynamic unity of the Divine, so that ultimate yet dynamic harmony can be achieved within man and within the universal cosmos in a dimension beyond our comprehension. The structure and world of the Sefirot found a fascinating visual illustration using the Menorah as a structure of the Sefirot.

The supreme rank attainable by the soul is conceived in the Jewish mystical concept of Devekut, cleaving to God. This concept is primarily linked with the concept of love which is reciprocal ("and ye shall cleave unto Him," [Deuteronomy 13:5]), and with the concept of awe, and does not lead to "union" with God but to close "attachment."

Man's psyche longs for "light" and the fear of the "unknown" throughout life is experienced as fear of the "dark." This fear is intensified - even to a degree of panic - in illness, aging and facing death. Man with faith or seeking faith throughout his life has an inner torch whose battery is always ready to be recharged. Also man without faith finds a torch through his life instinct, which clings to "hope" based on encouragement and medical perseverance. But when these fade, he feels abandoned. Man with faith or seeking faith has received and is surrounded by "light" signals which radiate throughout his inner being as he is linked with the Divine destiny of man's inner pilgrimage. This approach - even if viewed only as a "psychic fact" - creates an inner dynamic which harnesses more than man's physical and psychological strength as it lifts him on to higher spiritual resources, not in isolation, but in the trust and knowledge of being a link and part in the chain of Abraham's descendants and of mankind, on the "Ladder of Ascension" striving for spiritual fulfillment.

The symbol of the "Ladder of Ascension" has a special place in Jewish and universal religious contemplation and literature. Various interpretations and their significance are inspiringly illuminated by my brother, Alexander Altmann, in his Studies in Religious Philosophy and Mysticism (1969, pp. 41-72).

Carl Jung's term of "psychic fact" becomes a helpful tool for comprehension on the psychological level of understanding. It loses its limiting aspect when the experience of sharing and recognizing the "psychic fact" in others leads to an inte-

153

grated, higher, spiritual comm-Unity with the others, and with the unifying concept of God, symbolized by the Divine light.

Man's innate longing for "light" is experienced - in the agonies of incomprehension and incomprehensibility of the unknown - as a spiritual message, as a spiritual messenger, and as a spiritual path and bridge. This light transforms existence and mere contemplation into a dynamic creative "yes" to life, to the deep love and joy of life, the joy of unfolding the mysteries of the great potential of the human heart as the center of being and giving.

Throughout my life I was inspired by the Psalmist's words which my father (Chief Rabbi Dr. Abraham (Adolf) Altmann, of Trier, Germany) loved and with which he so often inspired his community on the Day of Atonement.

"Or zaruah latzaddik uleyishrey lev simcha" (Psalms 97:11).

"A light is sown to the righteous and to whom is of noble heart: joy."

I hope my meditation is an echo in response to the spirit expressed by the Psalmist, lived by my saintly father and mother and reflected in the wide range of his inspring writings.

A Thought of Consolation for Man

Perhaps man and all animated creatures have one great and comforting consolation in dying, when their transitory "entity" is being dissolved.

Just like the apple as a growing, ripening and ripened fruit of a tree enjoys the process of living as part of a big wonderful tree, knowing and gladly accepting the fact that its life has no separate, but only an integrated meaning, so also man should have the beautifying and elevating awareness of being part of the great, lovely and lovable "Tree of Life."

When all the excitement and fuss are over and the time comes that an aged and ripe apple falls from its tree, knowing that it means "death," he, at least, has the satisfaction of having contributed to the Joie de Vivre, the "Joy of Living" of his beloved "tree as a whole," and having a lasting share in the durable strength and happy existence of the tree itself. Instead of bitterly cursing death, he sweetens the death experience by blessing life, life in part and life as a whole; that is, his "own" life and the life of his "own" tree.

154

So also man should not face and meet his death in bitter, agonizing sadness and resentment, but look joyfully back to the days when he played a meaningful, constructive part in life as a whole, and allow himself to die with a great and blissful sense of satisfaction. Even when physically "fallen down," never to get up again, he should lift himself spiritually by the realization that the "Greater Life" which originated, developed and sustained him in a mutually creative love-relationship, is surviving him and going on forever, enriched and timelessly blessed by his living memory. It is not an anonymous, impersonally productive tree of life which keeps growing and growing in an automatic way, but a highly personalized and memory-inspired Tree of Life, with the names and pictures of each unique fruit invisibly engraved in its center-stem, its "heart, mind and very spirit of life" as it were. After all, it is and remains "Our" Tree of Life, the Tree of Life of each one of US and of US All Together.

Matching the Unfathomable Death Experience with an
Equally Unfathomable Faith and Courage

[Written at home in early September, 1983, after major cancer surgery and very limited life prognosis.]

I always wanted to die fully conscious and not asleep, facing death for what it really stands for and not missing the great metaphysical experience of my transition from life to what lies behind and beyond it.

Now I have been granted an extended time, to prepare myself for the end and the great unknown, and to be conscious of my approaching destiny realistically and with a keen sense of taking my departure from this world "seriously" and not only theoretically and evasively.

This is a great challenge for developing an entirely new attitude of life and death confrontation, which will be helpful and encouraging, even inspiring not only to me, but perhaps also consoling and uplifting to others facing the same or similar "terminal" situations.

There is a science and art of fearless living, but there is also a by-far greater science and art of fearless dying, matching the unfathomable greatness of the death-experience and realization of one's terrifyingly unknown fate after life, with an infinite and transcendental kind of courage. There is a "Meta-Reality" probably not only beyond time and space, but also beyond logical causality and logical reason and purpose.

Just because of the great, incomprehensible and impenetrable mystery of death, there is all the greater hope that there
155

is a meta-rational destiny in store for us; so wonderful and rewarding that it is "out of the" world of human understanding, imagination or dreamy fantasy. Therefore it is no wisdom to give in to despair, fearfulness and negative thoughts, feelings and guessings facing death.

On the contrary, one should meet death smilingly and blessingly rather than cursingly, hoping that it is in the nature of the big "transcendental leap from life" to "beyond-life" that there must be the unspeakable experience of "disruption" rather than "smooth continuation and transformation" in the sense of a painless metamorphosis.

Pain Experience and Spirituality

[Dictated personally by Erwin Altman to his brother Manfred on May 8, 1985 during the night, in the midst of agonizing pains and during a long period of continuing inability to sleep due to these pains. No drugs could help.]

Many times we experience in life little or bigger kinds of death. Pain experience is a part of death experience, as pain is related to death. If we would find ways and means to alleviate the suffering, the horror, and the agony of pain without creating unconsciousness, this would add a new chapter of living. The Prophets have seen the close connection between death and pain and anticipated the realization of this dream of dreams. Also the Psalmist visualizes keenly and joyfully the time when all agonies of pain will be converted into joy and song.

But there is one important thought which should not be missed in this search.

Joy and happiness as a goal of life are only incidental byproducts of a much greater challenge and goal which expands and transcends both the idea of abundant happy satisfaction and the idea of its absence, the opposite of contentment.

There is a Beyond Reality which extends and transcends both the positive and negative aspects of life's fulfillment and experience.

The task is to find a way beyond joy and sadness, even beyond life and death. Only in this 'Beyond' lies the key to the understanding of what far exceeds positive and negative aspects of living and dying. The Stoics have tried to reach the point in their life-attitude which exceeds pain and pleasure. However, they have gone too far and were too one-sided in their approach. Their efforts ended in failure, as

156

they became too radical and one-sided one way or the other.

There is, however, an uncharted land between pain and pleasure which is beyond the usual experience but nevertheless exists.

Only if we penetrate the secret which lies between pain and pleasure will we be able to rise above both.

The only remedy of overcoming pain, grief and sadness is by taking the reality of a third inner experience seriously and making it goal-worthy. For this it is important to realize that there is more than the experience of "I." The greatest redemption of man lies in the clear recognition of and personal direct meeting with that "Beyond I" dimension. And even in the greatest and most personal struggles and trials and tribulations of pain, this most personal and intimate need-situation can lead to this challenge. Man will not succeed in relieving distress if he remains unaware of this greater dimension. The way is by breaking through the frontiers and limited horizon of the familiar "I." There is a Beyond Consciousness which far exceeds the subconsciousness and unconsciousness and comprises the Great Beyond of either personal and impersonal association with the new Identity of the "Beyond I."

It takes great courage and inner vision to truly realize this unknown land of Superior Reality. There are no master charts available and it can only be found from within and not from without.

But just like America existed long before its discovery, so the New Earth and New Heaven of Inner Outlook exist and aspire to come into the open as the great challenge beyond our individual time.

Perhaps this chapter of my Reflections might be called "Compensation and Direct Confrontation with Pain and Suffering" from my present Notebook of my daily and nightly outcries from pain and suffering!

[Continuing:]

It dawned on me, some day there might be a reason for my stubborn survival. It is very strong and powerful and it occupies my innermost mind. This could be the realization of whether I might still have some very important unfinished business to do in this world. And it is this business which is trying to push me from all directions to wake up and live up to those dutiful challenges.

It reminds me of one of the Adam legends, which our brother Alexander also mentioned, which might be pushing me in the direction of "do not slumber and sleep" (Psalms 121:4), because thy Master has commanded Thee.

Perhaps the calls of my Master which speak from my inner commandments and inspirations are too powerful a voice in me to find sleep.

It can also be expressed in the words of our dear father, which you and I often discussed, that the voice of Man's Inner Horeb (Revelation) cannot come to rest and final destiny before man's own Na'ase Venishmah ("we shall do and we shall understand" [Exodus 24:7]) have truly found their final self realization.

Perhaps my peace and rest will only come when the book of my duties Hasal Siddur Pesah Kehilkhoso (the order of the Passover service is now completed in accordance with all its laws) will have matched my pending Exodus from this world.

Perhaps my inability to leave this world as yet amounts to one great notice, that I have not yet finalized my highest and most precious duties in a literary sense, which could be a reminder to hurry up and to discharge my very personal commitments to a higher experience, to understanding and to an inspirational influence of a higher meaning.

Perhaps there is a very personal truth in the saying and message, "He slumbereth not and sleepest not - the Guardian of Israel" (Psalms 121:4).

There is a Guardian of Israel in each Jew, who powerfully attends to the task that no Jew should come to a premature death before he has fulfilled his commitment of higher testimonial witness in this world.

This whole beautiful passage about the Guardian of Israel can be interpreted to mean that whatever the need of Physical Man for sleep may be, the Divine part of Man, the inner Guardian of the quality of "Israel" in Man, of his Divine destiny, never slumbers; it is urging you, rushing you, inspiring you, constantly, vigilantly, not to leave this life before you have finalized your individual duties and commitments to the Divine, to God and His Plan. This inner higher voice protects not only our prolongation of life but also the quality of its final fulfillment.

Of course, physical man needs slumber so that the inner voice, which never slumbers, can be acted upon in the daily functions and tasks of living. Maybe, as these tasks are

158

reduced in the physical dimension - maybe we are meant to listen more, longer, to the inner Divine voice of the Guardian of Israel in us. Israel comes first and God will hold every Jew to this higher commitment. In a sense, a good Jew rests in peace only in association with the attribute of peace and rest of God. This is the special task and meaning of the "Chosenness of the Jewish People."

Spiritual sublimation of the pain experience needs to be rooted in the search for spiritual enlightenment. It leads to pain not to be taken so personally, to a sharing of the pain experience with Nature and its Creator; it becomes life's greater pain as a whole. Such sharing leads to a higher threshold of tolerance of pain, as one's higher inner self is allowed to lead to the inner experience of the "Beyond I" dimension. This is not auto-suggestion, not self-hypnosis; this field of spirituality and pain I hope to understand more and more, not only for myself but hopefully also as a blessing to others.

About my Expectations and Goals
at the End Stage of my Life

[Dictated in Room 4122 of Cedars-Sinai Medical Center, Hospice Unit, June 18, 1985, 20th hour, when life prognosis was four to six weeks, by Erwin Altman to his brother Manfred.]

Realistically I feel, with my physical condition going down and worsening, that the level of real communication may go down; this may develop into a gradual, slow progressive ordeal.

My attitude is not of fear or anxiety, but my basic attitude is of realistic, down-to-earth acceptance of my fate without indulging or complaining in anger or negative thought, feeling and reactions. I want to remain cheerful and positive-minded as long as possible, making the best of the little that life presently allows me in terms of appreciation of life enjoyment.

I also hope that I will be able to be alert and mentally awake for meaningful communication and exchange of life stimulation and inspiration by and to others. And I fervently pray that my most precious source of strength, the love between us three surviving brothers in our family, Alexander, you and me, our lifelong mutual spiritual inspiration and closeness, exchanging our thoughts and experiences, may continue to remain the great undimmed lights of my consciousness and of the clarity of communication between us. And I always feel the immeasurable Blessing and Blessedness emanating from the eternal sacred memory of our beloved ones, especially of our saintly parents, our sister Hilda and brother Wilhelm.

159

Your continued loving presence here at my side, my dear Manfred, gives me - as throughout my life - your unfaltering trust, wisdom and encouragement, always in close union with Alexander.

And I pray that my level of ongoing free and so meaningful communication in spiritual kinship and friendship with Rabbi Levi Meier may be maintained fully, and equally so with my great doctor friends, my fine nurses and all relations and friends.

I even dare to hope that my mind and spirit of life will not be affected too much by the physical decline, and even increase to a certain extent, and a new period of illumination and enlightenment for the benefit of myself and others might be touched off in my final near-borderline phases.

I want to make the experience of dying as constructive and meaningful as possible and perhaps new horizons of reality and dimensions of existence will open up for me.

The more I approach the frontiers of physical living, the more I look forward, even with a sort of excitement and opti-mistic expectancy, to new spiritual vistas and avenues of promotional existence.

I am convinced that life is succeeded not by zero-nothing-ness, but by a new, far greater eternal reality of no-_thing_-ness, which hopefully is eternally joyful.

I also hope that my constructive attitude toward the ultimate meaning of having to go through pain and suffering will contribute towards the final conversion of all my trials and tribulations to infinite and everlasting joy.

So, I am engaged and involved in a double task: to reduce my pain and agonies of suffering to a minimum with the help of my doctors and friends, especially my family and - on the other hand - to increase my _tolerance_ of unavoidable pain to the maximum.

I hope that the wonderful institution of the present Hospice I am in will contribute greatly to the success of my highest aspirations in this direction.

My basic attitude is geared to retaining and even further developing a meaningful and inspirational way of living, as well as a dignified and even uplifting way of dying. You know my belief that the spirituality in us is the key to reach out beyond the pain experience into higher dimensions. This is my continuing great inner challenge. I believe there is reality

160

in existence beyond the concepts of living and dying, and life
and death must be approached in a holistic way, including both.

I strongly believe in Albert Schweitzer's "Reverence for
Life," but also in a profound and undying "Reverence for
Death."

There is a form of existence which is superior to life and
to death, as a matter of fact, even to the concept of "being"
and "not being," of some-thingness and no-thingness. There is
a "Ladder of Ascension," which is infinite in its unending
potential of spiritual growth.

I hope that this ongoing challenge of spiritual growth and
ever higher self-unfolding will give me strength and encouragement not to die as a pitiful victim of cancer, but as a joyous
victor converting even cancer from a potential "falling stone"
into a glorious "stepping stone" into higher realms of
existence in store for me and all mankind.

Meditation About the Last Shema Yisrael (Hear O'Israel) -
"Declaration of Faith"

Why is the Shema Yisrael selected as the last statement of
a Jewish person facing immediate death. Why - in the final
death-struggle - is God not called directly, but Israel is
addressed in the last message of messages? It is a double
accentuation and emphasis in the Shema on Adonay, not only in
the first mentioning of God's name, but also in the second.
This emphasis is deeply meaningful. In dying, the Jewish
person also repeats seven times (as at the end of the Ne'ilah
prayer on Yom Kippur) immediately following the Shema Yisrael,
the affirmation of God: Adonay, Hu Ha'Elohim, with the emphasis on Hu signifying that the unnamable God of the
tetragrammaton is God.

The Shema Yisrael corresponds to this exactly. It has many
equally valid interpretations and translations, but the recitation and proclamation of the Shema at the very moment of death
is probably meant in the sense: Adonay is our God from without
and within, Adonay alone! This testimony reflects the most
intimate direct relationship with God; man feels and realizes:
I am dying alone, as nobody can accompany me, where I am going,
I am "on my own," as never before in my life, but just in this
"alone-ness," which I am facing now, I am closer to God's
identity and His Alone-ness than ever before. In this true
alone-ness, I experience and recognize my very own Divinity
from within in the Image of God.

I realize the truth of "dust to dust," but I also realize
as never before, and testify to the truth: whatever is godly

in me will return to "God!"   I believe as a "Son of Israel" in
Adonay as my Creator and   my Redeemer, but especially this last
revelation-experience of "Godly lone-ness" I want to share with
Kol Yisrael (all Israel).

As the Five Books of Moses, which contain the Godly
testimony of His holy life, end with the words: Le'ene Kol
Yisrael, "before the eyes of all Israel," so a Jewish Tzaddik
and every righteous person dies before the eyes of all his
people, communicating with them in his last star-hour message.
Even in death he thinks more of the people he is leaving behind
than of himself.   And he passes from this world with an entirely selfless fulfillment of a Mitzvah: comforting, encouraging,
uplifting and inspiring the godly people of "Alone-ness," his
fellow Bney Yisrael - "SHEMA YISRAEL!"

References

Altmann, A. (1969). Studies in Religious Philosophy and Mysticism. New York: Books for Libraries Press.

Einstein, A. (1985). Ideas and Opinions. New York: Crown Publishers.

Hertz, J.H. (1943). A Book of Jewish Thoughts. New York: Jewish Welfare Board.

The Holy Scriptures (1985). Philadelphia: Jewish Publication Society.

Meier, L. (Ed.) (1986). "Morenu" Our Revered Teacher, Guide, and Counselor. A Singular Award-Ceremony and Tribute to an Outstanding Personality, Erwin Altman, J.D. Los Angeles: Cedars-Sinai Medical Center.

The Midrash (10 Vols.)(1961). H. Freedman and M. Simons (Eds.). London: Soncino Press.

Scholem, G. (1971). The Messianic Idea in Judaism and Other Essays on Jewish Spirituality. New York: Schocken Books.

The Talmud (18 Vols.) (1961). I. Epstein (Ed.). London: Soncino Press.

Selected English Bibliography of Books Dealing with
Psychology and Judaism

Amsel, A. (1969). Judaism and Psychology. New York: Feldheim.

Amsel, A. (1984). Rational Irrational Man. New York: Feldheim.

Bulka, R.P. (Editor). (1976-1987). Journal of Psychology and Judaism. New York: Human Sciences Press.

Bulka, R.P. (1979). The Quest for Ultimate Meaning: Principles and Applications of Logotherapy. New York: Philosophical Library.

Bulka, R.P. and Spero, M.H. (Editors). (1982). A Psychology-Judaism Reader. Illinois: Charles C. Thomas.

Feldman, D.M. and Rosner, F. (Editors). (1984). Compendium on Medical Ethics. New York: Federation of Jewish Philanthropies of New York.

Kahn, P. and Naiman, C.S. (Editors). (1983). "Behavioral Sciences and Mental Health," Proceedings of the Associations of Orthodox Jewish Scientists. Volume 7. New York: Sepher-Herman Press.

Klein, D.B. (1981). Jewish Origins of the Psychoanalytic Movement. New York: Praeger.

Ostow, M. (Editor). (1982). Judaism and Psychoanalysis. New York: Ktav.

Spero, M.H. (1980). Judaism and Psychology: Halakhic Perspectives. New York: Ktav and Yeshiva University Press.

Spero, M.H. (Editor). (1984). Psychotherapy of the Religious Patient. Illinois: Charles C. Thomas.

Spero, M.H. (1986). Handbook of Psychotherapy and Jewish Ethics. New York: Feldheim.

Spiegelman, J.M. and Jacobson, A. (Editors). (1986). A Modern Jew in Search of a Soul. Arizona: Falcon Press.

Glossary of Hebrew Terms

Adonay	One of the names of God.
Adonay Hu Ha'Elohim	The last declaration of faith on the Day of Atonement.
Ain Sof	A Jewish mystical concept referring to infinity.
Akeda	The episode dealing with Abraham's potential sacrifice of Isaac.
Aninut	The state of being an <u>onen</u> (see <u>onen</u>).
Atzeret	The conclusion of a holiday.
Aveilut	The state of mourning.
Ayin	A Jewish mystical concept referring to No-<u>Thing</u>-Ness.
Azazel	A sacrifice which is sent to the wilderness as part of the service of the Day of Atonement.
Berakhah	A blessing.
Berekhah	A spring of water.
Bney Yisrael	The Children of Israel.
Derekh Eretz	Literally it refers to "the way of the land" and figuratively, it refers to kindness and respect.
Devekut	A Jewish mystical notion referring to "cleaving" to God.
Ezer	A helpmate.
HaIvri	The Hebrew person.
Halakhah	Jewish law.
Halakhic	In accordance with Jewish law.
Hasidic	An 18th century movement which stressed the ordinary person's way of reaching God.

165

Hok	A statute, i.e., a Jewish law whose reason has not been revealed.
Horeb	The mountain where God's Revelation took place.
Hukkim	Plural of Hok.
Ivri	A Hebrew person.
Kabbalah	Jewish mysticism.
Kavannah	Appropriate intention in the performance of commandments.
Keriah	The rending of a mourner's garment.
K'negdo	Literally, "in opposition to."
Lekh Lekha	"Go forth."
L'Hayyim	A salutation, literally "to life."
Lifnim Mishurat Hadin	Doing an act which is considered "beyond the letter of the law."
Magen David	The Shield of David or the Star of David.
Mikvah	A ritual bath.
Mitnagdim	An 18th century movement which emphasized scrupulous observance of Jewish law, in contradistinction to the Hasidic movement.
Mitzave	A Divine law-giver.
Mitzuve	A recipient of Divine law.
Mitzvah	A commandment.
Mitzvot	Plural of mitzvah.
Mohel	A person who performs a ritual circumcision.
Molech	A pagan idol to which children were sacrificed.

166

Morenu	A distinguished title, meaning "our revered teacher."
Mushlam	A complete and perfect state of affairs.
Ne'ilah	The last prayers which are recited on the Day of Atonement.
Ner Tamid	The eternal light.
Olam Katan	The world in microcosm.
Olot	Sacrifices that were completely burned.
Onen	A mourner whose dead relative has not yet been buried.
Pardes	Literally, it refers to "paradise" and figuratively, it refers to a study of philosophy and mysticism.
Pesach	Passover.
Rishonim	Early medieval authorities on the Talmud.
Sefirot	A Jewish mystical notion referring to different paths of the soul.
Shaatnez	A statute regarding the fiber and composition of clothes.
Shavuot	Pentecost.
Shekhinah	The Divine Presence.
Shema	Refers to the Jewish declaration of faith.
Shema Yisrael	Literally it means "Hear, O' Israel" and figuratively, it refers to the Jewish declaration of faith.
Shmini Atzeret	The conclusion of the holiday of Tabernacles.
Shofar	A ram's horn which is blown on the Jewish New Year.

167

Sukkot	The holiday of Tabernacles.
Tallit	A prayer shawl.
Tamim	Whole, without imperfection.
Tefillin	Phylacteries.
Tzaddik	A righteous person.
Tzel	Shade or shadow.
Tzelem	Image, as in the Image of God.
Vav	The 6th letter of the Hebrew alphabet.
Viduy	A confession.
Yada	To "know" one's spouse in an intimate manner.
Yizkor	In memoriam.
Yom Hashoah	Holocaust Remembrance Day.
Yom Kippur	The Day of Atonement.
Yom Tov	Refers to Jewish holidays.
Yud	The 10th letter of the Hebrew alphabet.
Zekhut Abot	The merits of our fathers.
Zekhuyot	Meritorious acts.

HaLevi, Y., 82, 85

Hasidic, 60

Heschel, A., 127

Heteronomous, 27

High Holidays, 57, 60, 134,162

Hukkim, 82-86

Identity, 86

Islam, 78-79

Israeli, I., 76

James, W., 16-17,56-57, 59

Jerusalem, 8

Job, 96-106

Judaism
    Orthodoxy, 59
    Reform, 59

Jung, C., 27,74 , 96-106, 154

Kabbalah, 103-106, 153

Karo, J., 26

Kent, C., 91

Kierkegaard, S., 16

Kubler-Ross, E., 134

Kurzweil, Z., 51

Ladder
    of Ascension, 49, 140,149,153,161

Laing, R., 15

Lamm, N., 50-51

Law
    Jewish, 54

171

173

* This General Index includes significant themes and names. Names of authors cited in references or bibliography are not listed.

The Bible

Leviticus	Pages
9:3	5
16:7,8	104
19:2	7,12,33
19:3	13
19:14	72
19:17	69
20:26	21,82,85
23:40	109

Numbers

14:17	121
20:20	130
23:9	83
23:19	127
28:26	44
33:38	127

Deuteronomy

4:6	82,85
4:19	77
5:22-25	61
6:18	7
7:6-8	146
7:7-8	77
7:24	128
12:1-4	80
12:28	128
13:5	153
16:15	109
17:10	64
22:3	91
26:40	109
28:9	10
34:5	127
34:8	130

Joshua

24:3	79

Samuel I

25:29	147

The Midrash*

Genesis	Pages	Leviticus	Pages	Numbers	Pages	Deuteronomy	Pages
9:5	123	9:3	5	25:11	10	34:5	128
12:3	148	19:14	72			(Sifre)	
26:5	4	20:26	21,82,85				
32:5	4		(Sifra)				
42:8	79						

*All citations are from Midrash Rabbah unless otherwise indicated.

The Mishnah

Moed Katan	Pages	Sanhedrin	Pages	Abot	Pages
3:6	44	4:5	75	2:2	131
				2:10	119
				3:17	5
				4:2	97
				4:17	128
				5:21	124
				5:23	26

The Babylonian Talmud

Maimonides

The Guide of the Perplexed	Pages
2:25	34
3:22	105
3:23	105
3:31	85
3:32	29

Mishneh Torah	Pages
Yesodei Hatorah	
2:1	27
Deot	
1:5	10,11
6:6,7	69,70
Teshubah	
2:8	131
3:1-4	70
7:2	119
Keriat Shema	
2:8	33
Yibbum	
8:12, 13	33
Issure Biah	
21:11	33
Sanhedrin	
24:10	34
Edut	
9:10	34
Melakhim	
8:11	77
11:1	29
11:4	27,78,85

Zohar

Shulhan Arukh

About the Author

Levi Meier, Ph.D., is Chaplain at Cedars-Sinai Medical Center and a psychologist in private practice in Los Angeles, CA. He received his M.S. in gerontology and Ph.D. in psychology from the University of Southern California. Rabbi Meier was ordained at Yeshiva University where he received an M.A. in Jewish Philosophy. Through his varied and extensive clinical and educational background, he serves interchangeably as rabbi, psychologist, gerontologist and thanatologist.

Jewish Values in Psychotherapy is a sequel to his first book, Jewish Values in Bioethics, which was selected as Jewish Best Seller by the B'nai B'rith International Jewish Monthly. He and his wife Marcie live with their four children in Beverly Hills.

183